What Leaders are Saying

This is a brilliant and masterfully crafted aspirational story that brings a refreshing perspective of what is possible in today's classrooms and larger communities with the challenges that characterize our learning environment. As a 30-year educator who has served roles as a teacher, site administrator, and at central office, I have come across many educational books with great tips, recommendations, and promises of success. However, I have never read one that walks the reader through how to expertly leverage mindfulness practices, social-emotional support, and district office resources that successfully transition families into the school system as well as create an ecosystem for them to thrive 365 days a year.

As a central office administrator on executive cabinet, it is oftentimes challenging to feel as though you are making a direct impact on students and the community. This story has empowered me with a renewed vision of how our school communities can operate and function, drawing from common sense practices of shifting systems to serve our families and students holistically. This is a roadmap to transform the lives of students, to set up staff for successful encounters with students and families, and to guide community partners in creating sustainable systems that outlast us all.

Dr. Tonia Causey-Bush, Assistant Superintendent, Academic Services, Banning Unified School District

The Education Imperative accepts the premise that our education system must do better because our nation and all children deserve more. Rather than dwell on the many problems facing American education, author Charles Wright Jr.'s novel tells a story of what's possible when a community comes together to create bold change. His solutions are built on a systems approach that invites stakeholders to embark on a collective journey, committing to a transformational process aimed at achieving success for all students, families, and communities.

The author's proposed transformative process is informed by a lifetime of personal experiences living and working inside and outside school systems in different areas of the country. He has put the critical pieces together to create a vision of an integrated and sustainable school system that works for all students. I encourage you to use this book as your tool to take the success journey with other stakeholders. It is extremely ambitious and will challenge you to think and act differently to achieve better outcomes. Our nation's future is in the balance, and the time for action is now.

Joe Aguerrebere, Former President, National Board
for Professional Teaching Standards

Throughout my career, I've read several education reform books, many claiming to have the 'solution' and others providing formulas for success without acknowledging issues of context and equity. *The Education Imperative* has taken a unique approach in combining fiction and non-fiction to allow readers to reflect on their experiences and question processes as they wonder through the eyes of real-life situations. Charles acknowledges the complexity of systemic reform and offers a tool to explore each community's journey to provide individualized support and services.

Dr. Ana Tilton, Former Executive Director,
Grantmakers for Education

A remarkable, courageous offering to a society and system in desperate need. Not only has the author maintained hope after thirty-plus years of witnessing worsening outcomes in Education, he is offering a transformative, interdisciplinary-informed, community-driven vision that I believe will captivate and empower the hearts and minds of those who have the power to co-create thriving ecosystems.

As a retired school counselor, I was in the trenches with students like the ones in this story, operating alongside under-resourced teachers and parents, and working myself to the bone for outcomes that still did not meet the needs of the children I supported. Today, as a grandmother, I am grateful for thought leaders like Charles who are determined to treat students and staff as whole human beings with needs that have been overlooked by our systems for far too long.

My prayer is that the leaders who pick up this book will agree to meet on the sacred grounds of our contractual obligation to our children, those who support them, and our future.

Sandy Ingle, PsyD, Retired School Counselor

As a Law of Attraction author who's written extensively about new paradigms and their power to help us change, and a recently retired public school administrator who had front-row seats to the need for change in public education, I highly recommend the approach Charles Wright, Jr. is taking with this book.

The Education Imperative offers an innovative paradigm for education that meets the needs and nurtures the potential of every stakeholder. Through the aspirational story, his insights into the mindsets, incentives, and other invisible barriers to change, and reflective questions, readers are invited to learn, probe, and hold themselves and their school system leaders accountable.

If you're open to new paradigms in education that will result in significantly better academic, behavioral, health, and life outcomes for students, parents, teachers, administrators, and staff, this is a must-read.

Greg Kuhn, Retired Public School Administrator, Author and Speaker

For nearly two decades, I have worked closely with central office and school leaders in urban and suburban school districts as a data strategist and nonprofit executive. *The Education Imperative* offers a perspective on public education that is sorely needed, one infused with optimism and hope for a better tomorrow. The author, Charles Wright, Jr., doesn't shy from naming the headline-making statistics, but addresses them with a rousing vision of what could be, given thoughtful and dedicated strategy, collaboration, and innovation.

This story of a family, a district, and a community coming together to enable all students to thrive is thought-provoking and pushes the reader to reconsider so many of the ideas and assumptions we take for granted about what public schools can achieve. *The Education Imperative* offers a beacon for those education stakeholders who are seeking a path for the change they suspect is possible.

Anyone who has a stake in public education and its outcomes—teachers, administrators, staff, parents, and communities—will find this book inspirational and empowering, offering the message that we can realize the promise of schools as incubators of opportunity for all students.

Cori Stott, Administrative Director of the Digital Wellness Lab (DWL) at Boston Children's Hospital

The Education
IMPERATIVE

for Leaders Working in and with Central Office

A Tool for Transforming Your
District Community into a Thriving Ecosystem

CHARLES E. WRIGHT, JR.

Saved By Story

The Education Imperative

for Leaders Working in and with Central Office

A Tool for Transforming Your District Community
into a Thriving Ecosystem

Published by
Saved By Story Publishing, LLC
Prescott, AZ

www.SavedByStory.house

Cover by Alyssa Noelle Coelho
Interior Design by Dawn Teagarden
Photo/Illustrations by Kriss Wittmann

Library of Congress Control Number: 2023907862
Paperback ISBN: 979-8-9869578-9-0
eBook ISBN: 978-1-961336-99-5

Printed in the United States of America

www.SavedByStory.house

To my late parents, Charles and Virginia Wright.
I am grateful for your unwavering love, support, and guidance.

To the students, teachers, principals, parents, central office leaders and staff, community organizations, and local, state, and federal agency teams who strive and sacrifice to make the existing systems work and yearn for a better public K–12 schooling experience and work environment that produces better outcomes for students.

Acknowledgments

First and foremost, to my wife, Stephanie, and daughter, Sadira, thank you for your constant support and love, and the lessons you continue to teach me along my journey.

The vision, learnings, and ideas expressed in this book were informed and refined by the input of many valued colleagues. I am grateful to each of you for generously sharing your time and expertise.

A huge thank you to the individuals who read early drafts of my manuscript and provided constructive and helpful feedback: Joseph Aguerrebere, Sanda Balaban, Tonia Causey-Bush, Ashley Davies, Niki Elliott, Maria Gingerich, Brenda Hodges Howell, Julie Pham, Randy Kahn, Don Kennedy, Melissa Ross, Cori Stott, Ana Tilton, Harium Martin Morris, Barbara Robbins, Allison Wood, and Stephanie Wright. I am grateful for your candid feedback.

Thank you to the Saved By Story team for your expertise, guidance, and patience throughout this process. I could not have done this without you.

To my late and dear friends and family members Joe Lanton, Ennis Cosby, Hugh Williams, Seana Stefan Lewis, Pa Williams, Grandma Dorothy, Grandma Carolyn, Aunt Cordia, Grandma and Grandpa Smith, and Uncle Bobby. Thank you for wonderful memories and the many ways you contributed to the journey that got me to this point.

To my teachers, mentors, friends, and colleagues over the years. Thank you for enriching my life and contributing to my growth.

Thank you to my many friends and family who have supported my efforts to promote this book. A special thanks to Robb Brown, Mary and Sidney Chambers, D'Andre Davis, Janice Mereba, Melissa and Jerome Ross, Alex Rundlet, Jennifer Sik, and Marcus Teague.

Contents

Finding Your Reader Pathway

My intention for this book has always been to create a tool that supports leaders with starting or accelerating conversations around transformation in their school district communities, but my definition of *leader* warrants early articulation.

After three decades in education, I believe that to create systemic transformation for our children, we must view every stakeholder as a leader—someone who observes what's not working and collaborates with others to discover and implement a solution.

I believe it's time for communities to accelerate and deepen their commitment to transforming our systems so that they produce fundamentally different and better results for all students *and* are healthy work environments for every adult who endeavors to make that happen. We have more shared influence than we are using, and my dream is that this book will activate the power within you to be a catalyst for transformational change.

What I know from years of experience is that each stakeholder comes to this conversation with a different set of experiences, knowledge, and insights and therefore needs to have these new concepts delivered in a variety of ways.

This book is best suited for those who have an intimate understanding of how central offices operate—superintendents, school board members, administrators, principals, philanthropists, researchers, etc.

If that is *not* you, I suggest you start with the e-book I wrote that shares the vision through the story alone, entitled *The Education Imperative: Ensuring Your Child Thrives in School and Life*. I hope it inspires you to create your personal roadmap for participating in making the case for transformation in your community.

If you are someone who has extensive school system interactions or knowledge, you may have some expectations of what you will find in this book based on other resources you've used. If after the first few pages, you find yourself wanting more conflict, research, or the "how-to," then I suggest jumping ahead to "Before We Get Started: A Note to the Reader" (and maybe taking a peek at the "About the Author: Why Does Transforming Education Matter to Me?") before you come back to the beginning.

The Call to Action

Phoenix County Commits to Bold Change

After reviewing all the stakeholder input, the Phoenix County School District Board's superintendent search committee crafted the summary below for the district background section of the job announcement:

We have been working for decades to address and overcome the district's systemic and structural inequities. While we have shown some signs of improvement, the transformational student and system outcomes we desire have been elusive. We believe this is due in part to instability and lack of continuity within our system, exacerbated by frequent turnover of those governing and leading our systems at the state and local levels.

Board members have heard countless stories of how students, parents, school leaders, community groups, and staff have to jockey and advocate aggressively to get the resources they believe they need to support their children, school, and programs because our processes do not consistently meet their needs. We recognize that some individuals are more effective and successful than others in this process and believe this reveals systemic and structural inequities. We understand how the persistence of these inequities has eroded trust between our school system and community, resulting in many polarized views.

We can and we must do better to improve student outcomes by rethinking and redesigning the processes that support them, starting with our school district! We envision a school system and supporting ecosystem where every expectation, practice, process, program, subsystem, engagement, training, and decision within it is developed to effectively support every student in a holistic manner to achieve significantly better academic, behavioral, health, and life outcomes. We refer to this system as a student-centered system. This is in sharp contrast to visions that focus primarily on students as learners or as it relates to their ability to direct their own education. Our vision of a student-centered system embraces a One System, One School culture that is unified in its support of students and adults getting the assistance they need to thrive. This system is a vibrant, collaborative, service-oriented workplace that fosters creativity and is considered among the best places to work. Our commitment to students compels us to form an ecosystem characterized by deep partnerships and alignment with the community-based organizations, agencies, post-secondary providers, and employers that support and provide opportunities for our students.

Evan Ellis, an education leader who had worked in school districts, the business world, and the philanthropic sector, learned of the vacancy at Phoenix County School District. He was excited about the board's commitment to transforming into a student-centered ecosystem and had the following thoughts as he read the job announcement:

I appreciate that the board and community seem to get that their school system isn't broken per se. It was simply designed for an era that doesn't exist anymore, and they've reached a point where they can no longer accept the incremental improvements in student outcomes their system is producing. I know the many efforts to meet the needs of students over the last several decades—federal, state, and local—have been programs and funding that have been injected into a system designed to teach to the middle, using a mass-production approach. Local, state, and federal governments and philanthropy have invested increasingly more money to get systems to achieve the evolving goals they set, without consistent student success at scale.

Reflecting on the type of transformation necessary, Evan began to outline the longstanding approaches he believed must be reconsidered during a transformational process to a student-centered system. If granted an interview, he would want to find a way to share these beliefs to get a sense of whether there was alignment with how he and the board thought about the change a transformation would bring. Below are his notes on the common beliefs that must be rethought:

1. It makes more sense for students to learn in a traditional setting where seat time in the classroom matters more than applied learning experiences or the degree to which the student has mastered the content.

2. The student archetypes[1] used to inform and allocate resources for programming (general ed, special ed, English language learner, advanced learning, etc.) are effective for achieving the best student outcomes.

3. Aside from illness, all students will attend school the entire day and school year, keeping pace with the planned curriculum.

4. Every good teacher is a good teacher for every student.

5. The neighborhood school should be equipped to meet the comprehensive needs of all its students.

6. Investing in teacher professional development and higher salaries are the most important investments to advance student outcomes.

7. Punitive discipline and grading practices are effective ways of motivating students and building readiness for the real world.

8. The pacing of content delivery and student learning is paramount in school and must take precedence over addressing the mindsets and traumas that teachers and students bring from their personal lives into the classroom.

He was ready to take on every one of these, so he applied for the job and shared his vision. As soon as they hired him, he hit the ground running.

Returning from a full day of meetings with parent groups and civic and community leaders, newly hired superintendent Evan Ellis paused in the doorway of his office and stared at his desk stacked with notes, reports, and presentations.

He took a deep breath as he walked over to his chair and dropped his worn leather messenger bag beside his desk. After unbuttoning his suit jacket and loosening his tie, Evan sat down with intention. He was unsettled about what he had learned today.

We have to do something bold to enhance the system's capacity to improve every student's life trajectory, he thought.

Opening his laptop, he began creating a discussion document that would highlight what he had learned from stakeholder interviews in the first sixty days as superintendent. He wanted to outline a path forward for addressing the community's aspirations and challenges.

His thoughts were racing as he mentally reviewed the data and recalled the stories he'd heard from students, parents, teachers, and community members, as well as school and district staff.

Students:

- "I hate going to school."
- "It's so boring."
- "I don't learn the way my school wants me to learn."
- "I used to love going to school when I was younger, but now I wish I didn't have to go."
- "We don't spend enough time learning about the things I think are interesting."

Parents:

- "I have five generations of family members who went through the district's schools, and I'm the only one who graduated. I don't trust that central office leaders care about helping my kids learn."
- "We've had a few teachers who saw the potential in my child and helped bring it out, but we've had too many instances where there was not a good fit."
- "My child is neurodivergent,[2] and it doesn't seem like the school is designed to support him."

- "The district is too hard to navigate! It seems like those with relationships get better access to services. It shouldn't be that way."

- "My child is doing well in their Advanced Placement (AP) courses. Please don't water down the curriculum."

- "My child is telling me how school and the curriculum are limiting his potential. When he doesn't like the two options he's presented, he suggests a third and that's not welcomed."

Evan was struck by the number of parents who had made sure their questions, concerns, and ideas were heard throughout his information-gathering process, whether it was by showing up in person at a focus group, taking part in a survey, writing op-eds, or sending a direct email to him, a school board or city council member, or their child's principal.

Teachers:

- "We don't have adequate resources to do what we're being asked to do."

- "We continue to be asked to do more, and we don't feel like we have an adequate voice to make a difference in influencing how the system improves or how we teach students."

- "Sometimes it feels like we're not part of the same team."

- "When I need help from the central office, it isn't easy to get it, and I don't always feel supported."

Community:

- "The district has a long history of inequities and disproportionate treatment of students of color."

- "The best programs seem to benefit primarily families with means."
- "We've tried for so long to be good partners with the district, but we aren't supporting them anymore until the board can get its act together."

As he reflected on the stories he'd heard over the last sixty days, he could feel the satisfaction, anguish, hope, despair, frustration, or sense of accomplishment conveyed by each person sharing their experiences.

How do I capture their emotions? Leaning forward, he grabbed a stack of papers labeled "Key Data." *What data can I use to put their feelings into context and build a foundational understanding of the issues we need to address as a community if we want to create a system that empowers, supports, and positions teachers and staff members to help all students reach their full potential?* His mind raced, searching for solutions.

Flipping through the stack of data, he pulled out a folder marked "Most Concerning Data Points," and a few immediately stood out:

Student Academic Outcomes. While there were wide gaps in student proficiency outcomes in math, reading, and science by ethnicity at multiple grade levels, as he dug deeper into the numbers, he realized that the aggregate number of white students not meeting or exceeding standards in core subjects was very close to the total number of students across all the ethnic groups.

Why is there not more discussion about the significant number of students in aggregate from all ethnicities who are not meeting or exceeding standards in these subjects? The determination that had compelled him into this leadership position simmered in his belly.

He wanted to find out the specific strategies being used to help each group of struggling students and how effective they were, so he could provide the community more transparency around what was necessary to help every student succeed.

As he continued scrutinizing the data, he noted that the district's weighted staffing standards model prioritized giving additional resources to the handful of elementary, middle, and K–8 *schools* with the highest concentration of students achieving below expectations receiving federal Title I funding (roughly 720). However, the model did not have a strategy for addressing the needs of the significantly larger number of underrepresented *students* (approximately 4,250) achieving below expectations eligible for Title I funding that were spread across higher-performing schools in smaller percentages.

Students achieving below expectations in high-performing schools clearly need more help. How can we do this without diverting resources? he wondered as he continued sifting through the stack of papers in the Key Data folder.

Graduation Rates. There were disproportionate graduation rates, with an 85 percent graduation rate as the highest rate for white students. He was troubled that the graduation rate for Native American, African American, and Hispanic American students hovered between 53 and 68 percent.

Digging deeper into the numbers, he discovered a similar trend that the 15 percent of white students not graduating translated into an absolute number that rivaled the total number of all Native American, African American, and Hispanic American students who were also not graduating in four years. Concerned that the narrative and strategies for resolution did not appear to intentionally include these students, his simmering determination turned into a rolling boil.

How can I reframe the conversation to create a greater sense of urgency and build more collective will for transformation without any one group feeling like their needs are not being addressed?

Student Health Survey. He flipped through charts that revealed rising anxiety rates, substance exposure, and other concerning trends in student mental health.

How are we helping students dealing with mental health challenges keep pace academically? Are our practices contributing to their mental health challenges? These questions gave him pause, and he sat back for a moment to consider their implications. *We have to do better,* he determined again and picked up the next stack of data.

School Climate Survey. These surveys, which capture student, teacher, family, and school administrative staff perceptions on topics that define the social and educational environment at the school, showed incremental upward trends. However, there was wide disparity between teacher and student views on whether the school provided a safe learning environment. There was also a disparity between students' views on school climate and parents' views on school quality. While only 60 percent of students said their school had a positive climate, 85 percent of parents were satisfied with school quality.

This seems off, he thought. *Why are the parents' perceptions of the school climate so much higher than the students? I wonder if parents are aware of their students' perceptions.*

After-school Engagement. One-third of parents said they were unaware of community resources that could help their child.

What are we doing to support parents who are not aware of resources in their community? And, are the students whose parents know about these resources thriving in the programs that their parents found?

Preschool Enrollment. The data revealed a gap in the capacity to provide quality preschool options. The district could meet only 40 percent of the community's preschool needs, and half of those classes had not adopted the full-day program, which was proving to be more beneficial to students in the long term than the half-day program. The community had the capacity to meet 25 percent outside of the school district, and the majority of those programs were still half-day programs.

How do we close the pre-school supply and quality gaps?

Teachers. Feelings of burnout and frustration were high in the annual teacher survey. In fact, teacher attrition was spiking up above its historical average.

We can't help students if we don't have healthy, effective teachers. I wonder what we're doing to address, even prevent, this problem. He made a note to follow up with HR and the teachers' union first thing in the morning.

School Leader Satisfaction Survey. The trends revealed that school leaders felt nearly two-thirds of all central office departments needed to improve customer services, clarify their processes, and provide more effective training.

We've got some work to do, he mused as he sat back in his chair and stared out the window, his mind sorting and synthesizing all the information.

As he reflected on the various data points, his conversation with a former mayor and foundation leader earlier in the day popped into his mind. The mayor's words were matter-of-fact: "The district's underlying issues have lingered for many years. There have been a lot of fits and starts and unsuccessful district-wide improvement attempts, but the last few years have made it clear that we have to change course."

He's right. The last three years of running schools remotely and in-person during the global COVID-19 pandemic have exacerbated long-standing inequities and brought many more teachers and staff to the point of burnout. So many have left, and many student outcomes have gotten worse, according to the Nation's Report Card data. We need to galvanize the community and its resources around a significant transformation. We have to work more closely with our community, agency, and business partners to help each and every student achieve outcomes that will prepare them for the next phase of their life academically, socially, and emotionally. Our system must show that it consistently listens, nurtures, and adapts, empowering staff and students to achieve their goals.

He recalled many teachers, community members, central office leaders and partners sharing some of, if not this entire sentiment.

To help him fine-tune his thinking on the scale of change needed, Evan picked up the phone and called his school board chair.

"Good evening, Kathryn. This is Evan. Do you have a couple of minutes?" he asked.

"Hi, Evan. Yes, I have about fifteen to twenty minutes before I need to get to a family gathering. What can I do for you?" Her offer was genuine, as usual.

"Thanks! I just wanted to share some of my high-level thinking on the first-sixty-days discussion document and get your guidance on a proposed course of action before I get too far into developing it."

"Great! I'm all ears." Evan could hear Kathryn settling in to give him her full attention. He imagined her curious expression and posture being fully focused on him as they always were when they were face-to-face, and he felt grateful again for everything that had transpired during the interview process. He, Kathryn, and the other board members had candid conversations about communication styles and the need for the board chair and superintendent to model the open dialogue and thoughtfulness desired within all board communications. They had already been building a strong foundation of trust and collaboration, which made this type of conversation easier to approach.

"I've talked with current and long-standing stakeholders, and I've reviewed data that point to remarkable accomplishments over the years. But I've also seen some notable pockets of organizational dysfunction and underperformance that contribute to outcomes that I believe we'd all view as unacceptable in a district and community that's committed to educating all of its students." He paused and took a deep breath while he waited for Kathryn's initial reaction.

"Yes, please continue," she responded.

"I've received a significant amount of feedback from parents, school and district staff, community partners, and civic leaders. The common theme that emerged is that the central office is seen as tone-deaf to the needs of their children and respective families. The feedback I've received was framed simply wanting me to be aware of their experiences and to voice their support for improvements in those areas."

He glanced at the stacks of papers on his desk and continued.

"I won't go into all the data now, but I've been examining the district's academic performance data, and it shows the absolute numbers of students who didn't graduate from the district within four years, and they're not great. What's more troubling is that the ninth-grade on-track numbers, third graders' reading proficiency rates, and pre-K enrollment numbers aren't pointing to a significantly different set of outcomes over the next four to twelve years for the existing group unless we intervene more aggressively." He paused again, giving Kathryn an opportunity to comment.

Kathryn offered her insight. "Well, since you announced your entry and learning plan, we have received more parent feedback across the demographic groups than we've seen in the past. Each board member has received a considerable number of parent emails with examples, all shared in the context of helping us understand the type of change needed. And the trend numbers you shared have been a concern of ours for some time. They are far from where we'd like to see them."

"Exactly," Evan agreed. "I'd like to get your sense of how bold I should be in presenting a vision to the full board and community that helps us transform our systems so that we can—with more predictability, regularity, and clarity—work more closely with the community to fully leverage its resources to support our students and provide a work environment that empowers our staff. Such a transformation wouldn't happen overnight, of course, and it will take a lot of relationship rebuilding. But I'd like your candid reaction to how the board and community are likely to respond to a discussion document that includes the exploration of such a comprehensive approach."

Evan paused and waited for his colleague's response, knowing that she had developed a deep sense of the community and board politics due to her willingness to connect with and listen to stakeholders and fellow board members. *She is a voice of reason,* Evan thought.

"I'd have to see the presentation, the language used, and the process for the transformation to have a better sense of how it would land. But conceptually, I know the vast majority of the board is ready for a significant overhaul of the district and wants to see more students—all students, actually—have success that prepares them for the next phase of their lives. The volume of parent testimonies and the clear examples they shared validated the urgency for a bold move to a student-centered system and, ultimately, ecosystem. We may have different views about what that looks like, and there will undoubtedly be those who are concerned about losing the things they've found helpful. But, I believe if you can show a process that will help us achieve what is important to us without that transformation partner trying to impose their views, you'd have a lot of interested ears. So, Evan, I trust your strengths in planning and communication. I suggest you develop the presentation using your experience and best thinking."

"Thank you, Kathryn," Evan replied. "I appreciate that vote of confidence. I'm planning to talk through the broad strokes of my findings and recommendations informally with board members and key stakeholders prior to the board work session. I think that will further inform my thinking and give any concerns or alternate ideas a chance to surface early."

"That's a great idea, Evan. And I'm happy to review any early drafts before you share them, if that would be helpful."

"Thank you. It will be. I value your efforts to help the board coalesce as one team, and your perspective on whether the discussion document advances that goal will be important. Okay, I'll let you get to your family function, and I'll be in touch with you on this topic again by next Friday."

After hanging up with Kathryn, Evan called George Abrams, president of the Phoenix Education Association. They had met a couple of times in Evan's first sixty days and had exchanged cell phone numbers. While they both expressed a desire to cultivate a strong relationship focused on improving student outcomes and conditions for teachers and education support professionals,[3] they didn't know each other very well.

To his delight, George answered.

"Hello, Evan. What can I do for you?"

"Hi, George. Do you remember when we last spoke, I shared that I'd like to have a conversation with you once I'd crafted my vision for the district based on my learnings from my listening tour?"

"I remember."

"Great! Well, I'd like to meet with you to discuss this when you've got some time."

The two leaders made plans to meet the following week at a quiet, off-site location, and Evan went to work preparing his presentation.

When the day arrived, Evan was ready. After greeting one another, they sat, and Evan got right down to business.

"I appreciate you taking time for this conversation. Our very first conversation has stuck with me." Evan opened his journal and then looked back at George. "I have five takeaways from your initial comments. First, while the work conditions at the district have been improving, there is still considerable room for improvement for teachers and education support professionals…"

Evan quickly ticked through the four remaining items George had previously shared, adding other relevant items that had been relayed to him and some that he had personally experienced.

"I'm glad you took note of my concerns, and I appreciate the candor of this conversation. You named several important areas that we both believe need more than a little attention. I'd like to see us make sustained progress in at least a couple of those areas," George replied bluntly.

"I agree. I have several ideas based on my listening sessions, and I'd like your support in amplifying teachers' and education support professionals' voices by engaging them in the process. I would like them to inform the approach and pace I recommend for driving change in the district."

"What do you have in mind?" George leaned in with curiosity.

Evan shared his ideas, and the two discussed them more in depth. By the time their conversation ended, they had developed a plan for engaging teachers and education support professionals in the exploration process, including a survey, focus groups, town hall meetings, and an advisory committee supporting the new ideas he was proposing, if approved by the board.

They parted ways, their next steps clarified.

George left the meeting and later shared his discussion with his colleagues. They appreciated the superintendent's approach and proposed path, which eclipsed the skepticism they had felt as a result of prior partnership attempts by previous administrators.

Meanwhile, Evan went back to his office, picked up the phone, and called a trusted friend and fellow superintendent to learn more about the organization they had chosen to support their school system community's transformation and the other ones they had considered.

Through research, Evan learned about the System Transformation Accelerator. Believing it would help the community attain the type of outcomes they aspired to achieve, he incorporated it into his observations and recommendations discussion document.

After reviewing Evan's draft discussion document, Kathryn was excited. Together, they made a few tweaks to help the presentation speak more directly to some of the long-standing concerns of fellow board members that Evan may not have heard in detail since he'd only been in the district for two months.

Over the next few weeks, in preparation for the board work session, Evan shared the ideas in the presentation informally with several stakeholders. He shared them with board members and other internal and external stakeholder groups with the goal of receiving feedback on his initial observations and thoughts. In addition to listening to input from students, teachers, parents, and staff, Evan made sure to include community leaders who represented each demographic community in the district, business and civic leaders, and leaders of post-secondary education and career opportunities. He also made a point to reach out to Clifford, the district's liaison in the state superintendent's office, as well as Barbara, a state board of education member from Atlanta, and the district's legislative delegation. Their awareness and support would be vital to ensure the district received the necessary waivers to support its transformation process. Using the feedback from the informal meetings, Evan refined his presentation so it spoke more clearly to the common threads of interest and support across the many different stakeholder groups. In his presentation, he included the common questions and concerns raised by the different stakeholders and provided a clear response as to how and at what stage in the Accelerator process those questions and concerns could be addressed (pre-entry, pre-acceptance, and post-entry).

At the board work session focused on the learnings and recommendations of Evan's 90-day plan, there was rich discussion. Board members found constituent awareness and support for the proposed transformation process compelling. They raised several thoughtful questions, informed by their constituents, about the need for total transformation and its implications for students who were already doing well. These questions sparked a deeper review and discussion of the data supporting the proposal, which board members found persuasive. In the discussion, Kathryn reminded her colleagues that the Accelerator's process would support staff and community with shaping any changes that would ultimately get approved by the board. Given the urgency and support for developing new approaches to supporting students, and the

Accelerator's approach, the board members who expressed concern did not believe there was a need to worry prematurely about adversely impacting programs and students. They felt there was a great deal to learn by working with the Accelerator.

During the work session, a couple of board members questioned Evan about the value of participating in the Accelerator when the district had so many similar initiatives already underway, citing initiative fatigue, which was a common theme in staff surveys. Evan listened to their concerns and appreciated the gentle nudge to verbally share with the broader audience what had been shared in the board materials and in prior informal conversations.

"Thanks for asking that question. We do have many initiatives underway, but none are like the Accelerator. The type of transformative change our community desires and that is necessary to better support all of our students, however, will not be achieved without a comprehensive, coherent approach that, among other things, helps ensure our many initiatives are positioned for success. I'm especially excited about the Accelerator because it will help us implement such an approach and facilitate results that we can't achieve by ourselves. For instance," Evan pointed to a presentation slide on the screen.

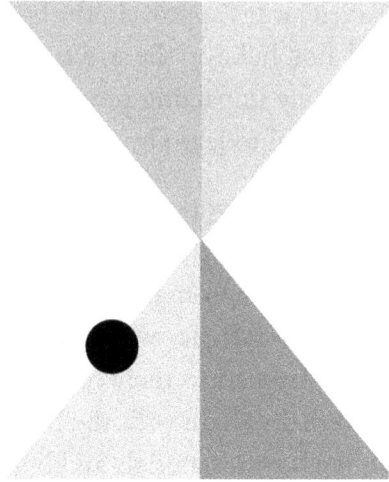

The Accelerator will:

- Enhance Our Capacity

"Our team has limited capacity. Half of the year, we're focused on the current school year. The other half, we're planning for the coming school year as we complete the current one. The bandwidth we *do* have needs to be maximized, and the Accelerator provides us with a number of supports that will leverage our limited staff capacity to accelerate our progress toward the long-term change we want for our community."

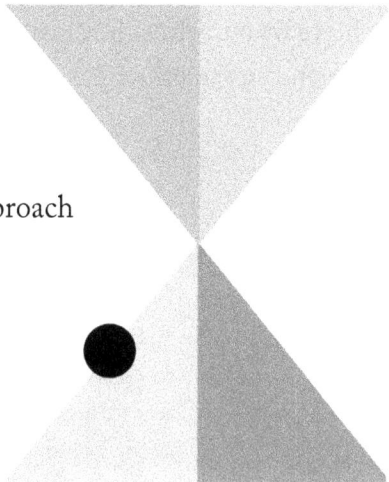

The Accelerator will:

- Enhance Our Capacity
- Provide a Structured Approach

"This approach is not focused on a specific set of programs. Think of it more like a general contractor for our transformation effort. They lay out a process, organize, sequence activities, bring together the necessary capabilities, and oversee the completion of the entire transformation effort on our behalf with our direction. Unlike a general contractor, the Accelerator connects us to funding sources that can help us advance strategic priorities when our resources fall short. The structure their approach brings is vital because we don't currently have processes in the district that help us maintain focus in the face of staff and board turnover, assess whether our programs and initiatives are positioned for success, ensure new staff understand how to navigate our systems to add value as quickly as possible, or incorporate change management into our practices to support staff with adopting new directions seamlessly and effectively. But by the end of this process, we will."

The Accelerator will:

- Enhance Our Capacity
- Provide a Structured Approach
- Create a Space for Us to Plan for the Future

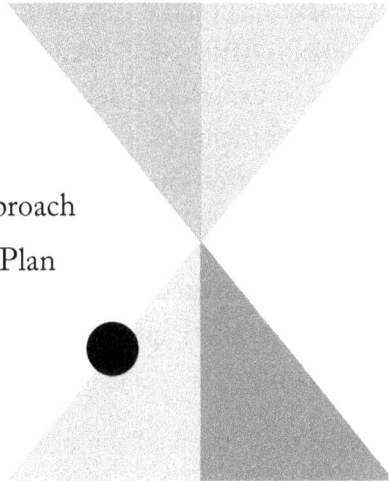

"Finally, we will have a dedicated space where our staff and partners can go to think freely and creatively, learn and adopt new mindsets, and develop the process and discussion materials that will be shared with the board and community each step of the way until our district has transformed to meet our shared vision. In prior years, Phoenix County School System, like many others, has taken promising practices from other systems without always seeing the results we thought we'd achieve. The Accelerator will help us consistently achieve the outcomes we desire by assisting us with transforming not only the way we work but also the mindsets and culture that have shaped how we work. I am confident working with the Accelerator will ensure we are laying the proper foundation to sustain and accelerate our transformation to a new ecosystem aligned with our vision."

"Thank you, Superintendent Ellis," the two board members spontaneously said, almost in unison. "Your response is very clear and helpful."

Another board member questioned whether the newness of the Accelerator posed a risk to the district if it failed to deliver on its promises. After some discussion focused on the Accelerator team's extensive experience delivering on a number of related promises, the board members were no longer concerned about the newness of the organization. By the end of the work session, the board had agreed to move forward with applying to the Accelerator.

As they completed the application process, they were very excited about what participation in the Accelerator would mean for their community.

When they received the notification that they had been accepted into the System Transformation Accelerator, they were delighted.

The story that follows is an aspirational composite account of what the district looks like the year after it completed its multi-year transformation work with the Accelerator.

Reflection is a Key to Creating Your Own Personal Roadmap for Transformation

**Set aside 45-60 minutes to journal.
Reflect, write, review, repeat.**

- What feelings and ideas emerged for you as read this chapter?

- Do you believe your school system has made a compelling case with key stakeholders for the change it wants to bring about through its strategic plan? Why or why not?

**Download additional questions at
www.EdImperative.org**

Is Phoenix County Similar to Your District?

In preparation for the superintendent interview process, the Phoenix County School District had held many stakeholder forums to find out what mattered most to the community. The information below is a synthesis of comments taken from those forums:

Parent Expectations of the School System

The paragraph below was written by the parent advisory committee, which was responsible for working with the search committee to develop and administer a parent survey as well as host a series of focus groups to learn what parents expect from the school system.

As parents, we all want our children to thrive in life. We expect our school system to be highly effective at providing our students with a foundation that prepares them to contribute to society. As such, we expect our schools to be warm, welcoming environments that spark our students' curiosity, cultivate their talents and joy for learning, and fill them with awe. We assume our schools will help develop our students' academic skills and social network, create and connect them to experiences that develop the soft skills critical to their employability, and model the empathy, compassion, and other attributes that are essential to their ability to thrive. We expect their learning environments will broaden their awareness of the many

27

careers they can pursue and provide pathways to a post-secondary opportunity or career that provides progressive growth and a living wage. We expect our schools and central office to be a healthy, well-functioning organization that develops and retains talented staff and leverages the community's resources. We also expect our schools and central office to be an accountable and transparent organization that maintains the community's trust. With this foundation, all families can send their children to school to learn what they need to know to grow and pursue their dreams with greater confidence that their expectations will be met.

While this was not the only view shared in the summary of parent feedback, it was the prevailing view.

State and School District's Educational Promise

The school board search committee prepared the following paragraph for the superintendent job announcement:

The State Department of Education, State Board of Education, and district school board have developed mission and value statements that reflect our commitment to educating all students—preparing them for post-secondary opportunities and to contribute to society. We believe all students can learn and eschew the notion that any individual is incapable of learning based on their race, gender, economic status, or physical abilities.

Broken Promises: Evidence Suggesting Transformational Change is Needed

Similar to your state department of education and local school district, the words in Phoenix County School District's and their state's mission, belief, and value statements form an important and powerful covenant between students, parents, the school system, and the community. This covenant suggests that each child who enters the school system will be prepared to compete for the post-secondary opportunities of their choosing when they graduate. While state regulations and district policies provide details that define the covenant, parents rightly expect regulations and policies to evolve to meet the needs of their children if they are not being met based on the mission and vision set forth. Families cherish this covenant because it sets the expectations they have for how their child will be supported as they fulfill their duties to prepare their child for life outside of their home.

Like today's education system, the reality for Phoenix County School District is that the covenant that exists between parents, school systems, and society is not simply to advance parents' or students' personal interests. It is a foundational element of their state constitution to ensure a productive workforce and a free society. When the original Department of Education was established in 1867, its primary role was to collect information on schools and teaching to help the states establish effective school systems.[4] It would be a hundred years or so before the anti-poverty and civil rights laws would catalyze the creation of an equal access mission that aimed to address the long-standing inequities that have existed in states. These laws further underscored that the covenant is a priority that must be honored as it is vital to children's future and their upward mobility in our society, as well as to the future of our society. The importance of the covenant to students, parents, and the community is no different in the Phoenix County School District community.

Unfortunately, the covenant has been broken for many parents and community members. Student outcome data shows that *school systems are not achieving success* with far too many students. For example, according to the 2022 Kids Count Report:

- More than 40% of all fourth graders in each ethnic group scored below proficient in reading on the 2022 National Assessment of Educational Progress. These outcomes alone should be sufficient evidence that comprehensive redesign is necessary to ensure all students' needs are met. However, signals that the systems are not working well enough get clearer. More than 59% of students in five of the six ethnic groups scored below proficient. The evidence gets even stronger, showing us that 80% or more students in three of the ethnic groups scored below proficient.[5]

- More than 55% of all eighth graders in five out of six ethnic groups performed below proficiency in mathematics, according to the National Assessment of Educational Progress. Nearly 40% of eighth-grade students scored below proficiency in the remaining ethnic group.[6]

- Nearly thirteen million children under the age of eighteen are at an increased risk of substance abuse and mental health issues, according to the National Survey of Children's Health.[7] Taking the fall 2021 public school enrollment for pre-K to twelfth grade (49.4M), approximately 26% or about one out of every four children at school are dealing with traumas that require great care to facilitate healing.

- Half (50%) of all children ages six to seventeen engaged in less than four days of rigorous physical activity (for a minimum of twenty minutes) in the past week, according to the May 2021 National Survey of Children's Health.[8]

- Nearly four million young adults ages eighteen to twenty-four are not enrolled in school part-time or full-time and are not employed part-time or full-time, according to the 2021 American Community Survey.[9]

From an academic, socio-emotional, and health perspective, the data suggests far too many students' needs are not being met by the current organization of and processes within our nation's school systems, despite the herculean efforts by many individuals at the school, community, central office, state, and federal levels.

To be clear, chronically low student achievement captured in the Nation's Report Card existed at alarming rates before COVID. The pandemic has only driven these rates higher. A deeper look at the percentage of students performing at or above proficient in key academic areas nationally and across the fifty states accentuates the need for thoughtful and immediate action toward transformation to student-centered systems. The table below shows a representative sample of students across systems participating in the National Assessment of Educational Progress, known as the Nation's Report Card.

Percent of Students Performing at or above the Proficient Level

	National		Low		High	
Reading	**2019**	**2022**	**2019**	**2022**	**2019**	**2022**
4th Grade[10]	34%	32%	24%	21%	45%	43%
8th Grade[11]	32%	29%	23%	18%	45%	42%
Math	**2019**	**2022**	**2019**	**2022**	**2019**	**2022**
4th Grade[12]	40%	35%	28%	19%	53%	44%
8th Grade[13]	33%	26%	21%	13%	47%	35%

Performance Range Across States

Performance Range Across States

Writing	National	Low	High
4th Grade[14] (2002)	27%	13%	49%
8th Grade[15] (2007)	31%	15%	56%

Science	National	Low	High
4th Grade[16] (2015)	37%	23%	51%
8th Grade[17] (2015)	33%	20%	50%

The National Assessment of Educational Progress shows persistent low outcomes in fourth- and eighth-grade reading and math in 2019, dropping lower in 2022 due to the impact of COVID-19. In fact, the 2022 fourth-grade scores reflect the first-ever score drop in math since the assessment began and the most significant fall in reading comprehension since 1990.

The outcomes in the Phoenix County School District are consistent with these trends, which necessitates fresh approaches be taken to achieve distinctly better outcomes.

The Wimbush Family Discovers Phoenix County

This book shares an aspirational story of one family's experience relocating to a new city and discovering a newly transformed school district. Phoenix County school district has organized itself and community partners around a holistic vision for achieving significantly better academic, behavioral, health, and life outcomes for every student. The district also provides better resources to the parents, teachers, families, administrators, and partners who support students.

Thus, the first chapter picks up *after* the Phoenix County School District and community partners were supported through the transformation process, which included:

- Equipping their leaders and staff with self-care and mindfulness practices that help them improve their well-being, personal performance, enthusiasm for their work, and student outcomes with the help of one of our partners, Mindful Leaders Project

- Resolving the underlying issues (mindsets, incentives, etc.) and working through previously challenging conversations that contributed to undesirable outcomes referenced in the Call to Action

- Mindfully examining existing processes and structures to address long-standing racial inequities (including their implicit biases), gaps in supports for students who are neurodiverse, and the need for a learning environment that promotes healing-centered engagement of students

- Using a mindful and healing-centered engagement lens to redesign processes for core services that impact students, teachers, and families

- Establishing routines for implementing and improving the use of new processes and technologies that support new ways of work

- Forging new ways of working with federal, state, county, and city-level partners to support the transformation process they have undertaken

- Creating feedback loops that allow them to closely monitor performance and the satisfaction of all stakeholders and make timely course corrections

The Mindful Leaders Project

The Mindful Leaders Project equips teachers and leaders with self care practices by teaching intrapersonal and interpersonal mindfulness strategies. The primary objective of their intrapersonal mindfulness strategies is to help the teacher or leader learn to self-regulate. At the intrapersonal level, individuals learn how self-awareness of their own Adverse Childhood Experiences (ACEs) score, nervous system triggers, and strategies for stress management impact how they perceive students, colleagues, or situations and become the unconscious drivers of their behaviors and the lens they use to see themselves and others.

The secondary objective of their interpersonal mindfulness strategies is to teach the scientific foundations that help administrators and educators understand the critical role that social engagement plays in nervous system regulation for both adults and children. At the interpersonal level, educators are taught how facial expressions, vocal tone, nonverbal cues, and positivity resonance shape students' brain and nervous system development. Leaders learn to become mindful and intentional about how they utilize these features in their interactions with students, families, and even colleagues to create accessible and inclusive environments that offer a sense of felt-safety to diverse groups.

We are excited about this work because it has the potential to make important conversations possible within school systems and their communities. It also has great potential to help educators develop a deeper understanding of what it means to help students "co-regulate" their nervous system and brain to increase social and academic outcomes.

This is the transformed school ecosystem that Mary and Sidney, a newly married couple with a blended family, find while searching for the right school and neighborhood for their two children who are falling behind in school. Mary's biological daughter, Kya, is eight years old and has been having a hard time focusing and finishing assignments. Her confidence is plummeting quickly. Sidney's biological son, Chris, is fourteen years old. Mary divorced a little more than a year before this story begins, and Sidney was widowed about the same time when his wife died in a car accident. The family has been living together in Los Angeles but is preparing to move back to Atlanta, where Chris lived with his mother until she passed away. He has had a difficult time since his mother died and is not only falling behind in school, he also appears to be falling into a depression. Mary and Sidney believe moving back to Atlanta and being around more people Chris knows will be the best environment to help him recover.

With this shared understanding of the setting, let's begin the story and see exactly how a district-wide transformation impacted the lives of two students, Chris and Kya, and the parents, teachers, counselors, and even school administrators whose mission is to support them!

While this book shows what's possible for all students by focusing on a blended family whose children are dealing with learning and developmental needs due to trauma and neurodiversity, school systems educate and support students with a wide continuum of academic and socio-emotional needs, language needs, living circumstances, geographic settings, and medical conditions, to name a few that are not specifically addressed in this story. It is important to highlight these needs as examples of the complexity that school district communities experience as well as the importance of designing coherent systems to ensure they are met.

Living Circumstances. Some students live in rural areas and others in urban areas and, as a result, could have very different access to resources. Some students live in very impoverished communities, rural and urban. Some students are being raised by grandparents. Some students are in neighborhoods that have limited enrichment opportunities. Some students don't have anyone at home who can support their learning.

Socio-Emotional. Some students come to school with a wide range of socio-emotional development needs, including the need to learn how their actions affect the feelings of others, how to regulate their own feelings and behaviors, and how to get along with peers.

Immigrant and Migrant Students and Families. School systems support families who are new to the US; are learning English for the first time as an elementary, middle, or high school student; don't have anyone at home who can support their learning; and are navigating all the challenges that come with being a recent immigrant. At the same time, they educate students whose families may migrate to another geography during different times of the school year for work.

Neurodivergent. Schools educate children who have brain differences that give them different strengths and challenges from people whose brains do not have those differences. Accommodating such needs often causes teachers to need to rethink long-time classroom practices and approaches to student engagement. School systems and state education agencies are still working to develop systems that better meet the needs of these students within programs under Individuals with Disabilities Education Act.

This story provides a vision for a system that can meet the needs of all of its students, and the Accelerator represents a process intended to help any system work through how to better meet the needs of every student.

Reflection is a Key to Creating Your Own Personal Roadmap for Transformation

Set aside 45-60 minutes to journal.
Reflect, write, review, repeat.

• What feelings and ideas emerged for you as read this chapter?

• What data or rationale do you find most compelling to justify your system's call to action? Why?

• In your view, who are the stakeholders who need to get the call to action for transformation to occur? Why?

Download additional questions at
www.EdImperative.org

A Note to the Reader

To ensure a shared understanding, I want to highlight two specific terms I use throughout the book. The school district, district, and central office will at times be referred to as *the system* or *school system*. Together, their community partners, including nonprofit organizations, city and state agencies, business partners, and higher education institutions form *the ecosystem*—a complex network of interconnected systems.

If you are reading this, you may sense that most school districts and their ecosystems are not meeting the needs of too many students. You may feel that something bold needs to be done to rectify this long-standing problem and hope to find some answers on the following pages.

After three decades of navigating education in multiple roles and perspectives—as a struggling student, a mentor to at-risk students, a frustrated educator, a program assistant, a portfolio manager and vice president of strategy, finance, and operations in foundations focused on systemic education reform, personalized learning, and continuous improvement, and a deputy superintendent of a large urban school district—I am more confident than ever that transformation is not only possible, *it's imperative*. I know that the story I have ascribed to my fictional characters, Sidney and Mary Wimbush and their children, can be a reality in school districts across the nation.

Also, to improve your reading experience, I want to share some of the decisions I made about the narrative:

#1: No Research

I did not provide research and evidence highlighting the range of examples on which the vision in this story is based. While I believe research is important, I do *not* believe it is essential to catalyzing the dialogue, decision-making, and the unrelenting action necessary for communities to choose to transform their school systems into the type of student-centered ecosystems that better support all students and supporting adults. As important as research is, the reality is that the infrastructure that ties academic and action research is underdeveloped, poorly supported, and not reliable enough to support a transformation of systemic practices today. As noted researcher Anthony Bryk writes in *Improvement in Action,* "[t]he overall body of program effectiveness evidence available to educators is very limited… If our aim is to close the aspirations chasm [of what we want schools to do and what they can do], this evidence base will not take us very far anytime soon."[18]

#2 Minimal Conflict

I didn't follow the conventional path of engaging readers in the conflicts experienced by the main characters. Many of my early readers, who have extensive experience in the current education system, found it difficult to imagine that new systems could create an environment where conflict was not the defining characteristic of the relationships or the most relevant part of the story. In fact, those who did not know me or my background questioned whether the vision was possible and whether I knew what I was talking about. As a former deputy superintendent, chief strategy officer, and chief accountability officer—three roles aimed at bringing about systemic, transformative change in three of the nation's largest urban school systems—I have had an insider's view of the opportunities, challenges, and conflicts that exist at all levels of a school system. With all that in mind, I am confident that transformative visions similar to the one outlined in this book are possible.

Rather than immerse you in external conflicts, this story is designed to *expose* internal conflicts within you given your experiences, which have likely left an indelible mark on your thinking and beliefs about what is possible. This is *exactly* the experience I hope you will have as you read the book because real transformation starts with each individual in the (eco)system noticing what is and isn't congruent with their school system's mission and vision and then working toward something significantly better.

Throughout the book, you will find prompts aimed at helping you unpack some of your reactions, assumptions, and beliefs, all of which are essential to developing your personal roadmap for being a catalyst of school system transformation in your community. As you reflect on your view of what is possible and the experiences that cause you to think or feel that way, what you discover will be an important element of your personal leadership narrative and play a vital role in your leadership journey. I encourage you to use the question prompts to journal as you read.

#3 Minimal Personal Experience

While I have incorporated many anecdotes throughout the book and share my personal story at the end, the main story in the book is not a personal account. I decided to create an aspirational fictional story based on stories and examples I have observed, experienced, and read about over the years. A narrative vision, I believe, is the best way to engage readers in what is possible for all students when a focused effort on transformative change to a student-centered ecosystem is completed.

#4 Focus on What's Possible More than How to Execute

Having an inspiring shared vision of the future (the *what* and *why*) is essential to generating the will and energy necessary to persist through the barriers (the *how*) that make transformative change difficult to achieve.[19] Such a shared vision should convey the type and magnitude of transformative change that is needed. For this reason, I have focused on *why transformation is essential* and *what's possible*, and I have intentionally left out *the how*.

This approach may frustrate some of you, especially if you prefer to quickly get to the frameworks, examples, and key takeaways that enable immediate action. If that's you, I encourage you to permit yourself to connect more deeply with the possibilities offered in this book and those you and your colleagues envision for your district before shifting your thoughts to *the how*. I invite you to join me in focusing on what is possible for all students.

#5 Intentional Organization

The story follows a family and all the stakeholders who support them throughout the course of a school year. Depending on your role and your personal experiences, you may have questions and even objections. You may experience a significant level of disbelief because the story is more positive than you currently believe possible. For this reason, each chapter contains an "Is this really possible?" section where I address some of the most common concerns and objections I have heard over the years.

In those moments of inquiry, doubt, or frustration with not seeing *how* it all comes to life, I encourage you to write down your questions or objections using the prompts provided in the book or additional questions I've included in a downloadable PDF on my website. I think you will find that the prompts in the PDF make for rich discussion among small groups if you are working with a school district, state department, or school system partner organization.

Now that you understand the choices I made for the narrative and why I made them, I hope you will be more able to relax into the book and glean value from it. It is crafted to be an experience that inspires and compels you to bring about student-centered ecosystems with healthy work conditions that can truly support the education of all children, every day, in engaging settings that even the adults find nourishing and stimulating.

Reflection is a Key to Creating Your Own Personal Roadmap for Transformation

Set aside 45-60 minutes to journal. Reflect, write, review, repeat.

- What feelings and ideas emerged for you as read this chapter?

- What does transformation mean to you?

- What type of change can or should happen faster to better support students and families?

- What belief or story, if any, do you have that stands in the way of greater involvement and contribution?

Download additional questions at www.EdImperative.org

Enrollment

Collecting Information for Student Success

"I guess our next step is to enroll the kids. Do you want to do that tonight?" Mary asked her husband as they began clearing the dinner table. It was Friday night, and the kids had rushed through their meal so they could go hang out with some friends they would be leaving behind when they moved to Atlanta.

"Sure," Sidney agreed. "Seems like a good night to do it. The kids are busy, and I'm not too exhausted from work this week." As he placed his dishes in the sink full of warm soapy water, he glanced up and smiled at his wife as she gathered the rest of the dishes. "Everything about this school district has impressed me so far. I'm curious to see what the enrollment process will be like."

"It's nice to be at this stage. After exploring all the public and private schools on our list, I'm really glad we found a public school system that has done so much to make sure children thrive," Mary added. "The superintendent's welcoming video made me feel very hopeful for Chris and Kya. Have you ever come across a district that promises, and appears to deliver, such personalized support for their students?" she asked. He shook his head to confirm her suspicion as he continued his task at the sink, and she moved to help him dry the dishes. "I've heard of homeschool communities that provide self-designed learning, but a large school district meeting the needs of every child? It's a little hard to believe, honestly. I wonder how they do it."

"Well, the kids have had a couple of years full of big changes, and this move is going to be another big transition for them," Sidney said. "I'm glad they'll be in a place where other adults will be paying attention and helping them succeed despite everything going on in their lives."

Mary's chest tightened with anxiety as she thought about their children's struggles. The loss of Chris's mom, a divorce from Kya's dad, and the blending of their two families. It had been tough for everyone, and they were beginning to see the effects in their children's expressions, confidence, and especially their performance at school. And despite their mutual vision for seeing their children thrive, Sidney and Mary didn't always see eye to eye when it came to solutions. While she felt he was more rigid around the need for discipline, which often created static, he felt she was too lenient.

Steadying herself with a deep breath while she finished drying the last dish, Mary said a silent prayer that this new school district would provide a fresh set of eyes on the challenges they were all facing and provide real solutions.

Sidney dried his hands on the other end of the towel she was using and smiled before kissing her nose. "You ready?"

She nodded.

"Great. I'll get the laptop."

Sitting down together, they both marveled again at the inviting website featuring pictures of kids, families of all ethnicities and genders, and clearly written content that told the story of how this district supported its families and community. Sidney quickly found the enrollment page and clicked on it. When it opened, the soft music that had played in the background on the home page got a little quieter, and they began to read the instructions:

In order to match your child to specific teachers, environments, support staff, and community partners, we collect information about your child's particular skills, interests, strengths, and challenges. Please give yourself thirty minutes per child to thoughtfully answer these questions. The more we know, the more we can tailor solutions to meet your child's and family's needs.

"Wow!" Sidney exclaimed. "Of course, this makes sense, but I've never seen anything like *this* before."

Their eyes scanned the section headings on the page: Parent Assessment of Your Students as Learners. Student's Responsibilities and Emotional Profile. Staying Informed and Getting Engaged as Parents.

"Incredible," Mary exclaimed, her upbeat voice expressing an unusual tone of disbelief. "I'm not gonna lie. I feel a little intimidated by the amount of information they're asking for, but I'm excited to think about our children being matched with the right people and environments for them to get the supports they need."

"Me too," agreed Sidney. "Let's do it. Want to start with Chris?"

"Sure." A feeling of relief washed over her. Somehow it was much easier to talk about his son—their son—than it was for them to discuss her—their daughter.

"Skills?" Sidney started. "Well, from his previous report cards, it's obvious that he's right at grade level in reading, math, and writing as a C student. I'm concerned though. He used to get some Bs before his mom died," he said as he scrolled to the next section.

"Motivation?" He glanced at his wife's face and let out a deep sigh that matched the worried look on his face. "I know he's not very motivated these days and doesn't seem to enjoy school anymore, except for being with his friends. And he hasn't been doing his homework on time, if he does it at all. I miss seeing him light up about things that used to pique his curiosity."

Mary nodded in agreement.

"We need to find a way for Chris to get help so he can heal and learn how to work through his feelings."

Mary nodded again. *How would that work?* she wondered.

He paused and took another deep breath. "But first, let's get him enrolled in school."

They answered the other questions about motivation and moved to the Self-Discipline section.

As they read through and answered those prompts, Mary remarked, "Chris would be an A student if he could learn to study with the same self-discipline he applies to mastering his video games, computers, and sports."

Sidney smiled and nodded in agreement as they scrolled to the next section, Resourcefulness, and noted Chris had a knack for finding answers to the questions that matter to him. "He's certainly comfortable asking adults questions and searching for answers on reputable websites when he cares about the answer." Sidney chuckled as he typed in their answer.

When they got to the Community Resources section, Sidney and Mary both went blank. They were moving into town and had yet to buy a house. They wanted to be in a community with programs and services that would be useful, but they had no idea where they would find a home. They were grateful that the system had a tool to help them find community resources and even more appreciative that it let them indicate what resources they might need in the event Chris and Kya had a need that couldn't be effectively met by one of their local programs.

As they read the questions about family supports, they digressed into a conversation about how important they believe education is, especially since neither of their parents had attended college and their siblings had not received the necessary support at school to achieve their goals either. They were determined that Chris and Kya would have better opportunities and outcomes, and based on the questions being asked of them so far, they were more confident than they had been when examining other school districts. After a few minutes, Mary acknowledged they were getting off track and brought the attention back to the enrollment form.

"Family Supports?" started Sidney. "Based on our schedules, I just don't think we have a lot of time to spend at the school or even help with homework. Learning my new job will take time, and I was told when they hired me that I'd be working long hours for the first few months."

"I'll have some time to support their transition. I can't interview and prepare for interviews all day, every day," said Mary. "However, I would like help strengthening my ability to support their learning and improving my ability to identify and navigate resources in our new community." She checked the boxes on the form for those two opportunities.

As they discussed their goals for Chris for the year, they found drop-down menu choices helpful in clarifying their goals. After reading the descriptions of the learning environments they had never heard of before, they chose the option they believed would be best for Chris from the broad range of in-person and remote options, including traditional, self-paced, outdoor, and self-directed. "He would probably thrive in an outdoor model," Sidney surmised as he finished that section.

Ten minutes had passed, and Mary needed a break. She pushed back her chair and stood up, smiling. "Let's have dessert!"

"Sounds good to me!"

A few minutes later, they were taking bites and scrolling through the next section—Student Activities, Responsibilities, and Emotional Profile. As they scanned the page, Sidney's eyes widened as he read out loud: "There are options for students who need extra supports due to demanding after-school schedules, students who are dealing with a wide variety of learning needs that can't all be addressed during the school day, and students who have housing challenges, significant medical needs, are returning to school after extended absences, who leave school seasonally because their families are involved in seasonal work . . . " His voice trailed off as they both read the long list of responsibilities and attributes students possess. "I had no idea school districts supported students dealing with so many different types of circumstances and learning needs."

"I agree," said Mary, focusing in on the form with that quizzical expression that always made Sidney smile. "Chris's main after-school activities will likely be basketball and robotics, but when I find a job, he'll be responsible for watching Kya after school."

Sidney nodded. "Unless we can find some convenient and affordable after-school activities they both enjoy."

The last question in the Emotional Profile section made them pause. They both wanted to make sure the school Chris attended was aware of his recent loss and grief so he could receive some additional support.

As they moved to the final section, Mary remarked, "I have never been asked how I'd like to stay informed and get involved during the enrollment process." Sidney nodded in agreement, and they both checked the boxes for the topics they wanted to be kept informed of. She wanted weekly updates on school activities and district news and expressed an interest in learning more about the Learning Options Task Force. He, on the other hand, requested monthly updates on the district's budget. They were grateful they could customize their interests and preferences. Sidney was looking forward to volunteering when he felt more comfortable at his new job and sharing his input when opportunities arose.

"One down," said Sidney, smiling up at his wife as he finished the last bite of cake.

Mary's chest tightened again. She knew it was time to talk about Kya.

Seeing the worried look on her face, Sidney offered, "Hey, I saw a video on the enrollment site earlier that discussed completing the process when parents disagree. Why don't we watch it now? Maybe it'll have some insights on how to navigate this together."

While he looked for the video, Mary took another deep breath and whispered, "Sure."

When he opened the video, they were greeted by Dr. Niki, an expert in mindfulness practices and founder of the Mindful Leaders Project. They quickly took in her genuine smile, carefully twisted hairdo, and matching spiral earrings and necklace. Neither could quite understand what it was about this African American woman and her voice that made them suddenly feel so at ease.

As she talked about how certain conversations can trigger fight, flight, or freeze responses, Mary immediately recognized that discussing Kya triggered what felt like a fight response in Sidney and a freeze response in her. As Mary watched the video, she tried the breathing exercise Dr. Niki was demonstrating and could feel herself calming down. When the video ended with the importance of setting positive intentions for children and encouraging the use of the Enrollment Support Line, Mary felt much better and was ready to make the call to the support line. "Great! Let's try it!"

It was late Friday, around seven o'clock, and Sidney didn't think enrollment support would still be open. But to his surprise, it was.

A woman with a soothing voice answered the phone. "Good evening. Thank you for calling. This is Ms. Jones with Phoenix County School District's enrollment support team. How may I help you?"

"Good evening, Ms. Jones. This is Sidney and Mary Wimbush. We just watched the video on completing the process when there are conflicting opinions or challenging conversations ahead and are reaching out for help. We just finished our son's enrollment form, but we still need to fill out our daughter's. Since we have some differences of opinion, we're hoping you can help us."

"I'm so glad you called," said Ms. Jones. "As parents who both love their child, it's not uncommon for there to be differences of opinion. My partner and I have them all the time, but we always manage to find a way to make decisions that make us both feel comfortable. I'm happy to help you. Let me start by asking you some questions to understand both of your perspectives, and I'll do my best to help you select options that represent both of your interests and concerns. Let me pull up your application. Would you repeat your last name?"

"Wimbush," Mary replied.

"In the top right part of your screen, you should see an application number," Ms. Jones continued. "Would you read that number to me?"

"Yes, it's AB13451," said Mary.

"Great. I see you are moving to town. Where are you coming from?"

"Los Angeles," said Sidney.

"Oh, how lovely! My sister's been living there for the last fifteen years. We visit a few times a year."

"What a small world," said Mary. "We have really enjoyed our time here."

"Wonderful. We're happy you're moving to Atlanta. I think you'll really enjoy it. Let's get started on Kya's application so I don't keep you too long." She paused for a moment and then began. "How would you describe Kya's skills?"

"Well," Mary started. "She's strong in some areas and weak in others. Overall, based on her report cards and standardized test scores, I believe she's just below grade level in reading and math, and far below in writing."

"Thank you," replied Ms. Jones. "Sidney, what do you think?"

"I agree," Sidney responded without reservation.

"Okay, when you have an opportunity, please upload Kya's previous academic records—report cards, standardized test scores—if available. This additional information will help us plan supports for her. It looks like Chris's records have not been uploaded yet either, so please include his too. I'm sure you have a lot going on with your move, so please do not let this add to your stress. You'll receive reminders to upload that information. There's no need to worry because your application will be complete, but some of our team members may not be able to provide the best planning support without that information. So, send it as soon as you can."

"I'll contact their schools tomorrow and get those records for you," Mary responded.

"Great. Now, let's move to motivation. How would you describe Kya's motivation, Mary?"

"I would say she's slightly above average in motivation. Her grades may not reflect it, but she wants to do well in school and gets really frustrated when she doesn't. Don't get me wrong. She's not the type to pursue extra credit, but it is important to her to do well."

"I see it the same way," added Sidney before Ms. Jones could ask him. "Kya is motivated to do well. When we get to self-discipline, that's where Mary and I see things differently."

"Thank you for sharing that, Sidney," said Ms. Jones. "I'd love to hear what you both think about Kya's self-discipline. Remember to do the breathing exercises Dr. Niki taught if you feel a fight, flight, or freeze feeling coming on." She paused to give them a moment to breathe. "Mary, will you go first? How would you describe Kya's self-discipline, and what experiences have caused you concern or anxiety with respect to how her self-discipline is perceived at school and elsewhere?"

"Kya is very active," Mary answered. "Some people want to say that she has ADHD (attention deficit hyperactivity disorder), and that she should be on medication, but I've been doing some research, and I'm concerned that there is not much known about the long-term effects of it. With so many kids being labeled as ADHD, couldn't the traditional schooling approach be the problem?! I'm uncomfortable about my daughter being on medication. I don't believe anything is wrong with her, and I don't want her to think anything is wrong with her either. Plus, I've read about lots of people who have had ADHD and have done well without medication. Now, when it comes to things she enjoys, her self-discipline is above to well-above average. Her social skills seem a bit behind other kids her age, but I'm not too worried. She enjoys making new friends."

"I understand," responded Ms. Jones gently. "We have a lot of parents who struggle with the same concerns and questions and feel the same way you do. Thank you for being candid." She paused for a moment. "Sidney, how do you see Kya's self-discipline?"

"Well, I agree that Kya struggles in school," he began. "However, I am concerned that she's developing a negative self-image because she gets in trouble and is not doing as well in school as she would like. It's hard to help with her homework because it often results in a meltdown. While we've heard about ADHD, we haven't done much research and don't fully know the pros and cons of medication and other approaches. I just feel like we need to do more research than we've had time to do. We both love Kya and want her to do well."

Mary could feel her blood boiling, but before she said anything, she heard the same soothing music they'd heard during the breathing exercises and Ms. Jones, in a caring tone, saying, "Thank you so much for sharing your perspectives. It might have been difficult to share them, and even more so to hear each other's. With your permission, I'd like to make a couple of comments. Is that okay?" She waited for their response.

"Yes," Mary and Sidney said in unison.

"Mary," Ms. Jones began respectfully, but with a tone that sounded like she was talking to a girlfriend she had known her whole life, "I have worked with many parents over the years, and many have heard something like what Sidney said as their mate saying they were a bad mother. Is that what you heard, Mary?" asked Ms. Jones.

"Yes," Mary replied.

Sidney's eyes widened in confusion and a bit of horror.

"He didn't say that, Mary. That's not what he said, Mary. I want you to take a few deep breaths with me, okay?"

Mary could hear Ms. Jones breathe deeply, and she mirrored her breathing. Immediately, she could feel her anger melting away, and a smile came over her face when Ms. Jones said, "Are you okay, girl? I'm not there with you, but my sixth sense went off."

Sidney observed quietly with a bewildered look on his face.

"Sidney, you may be a little confused right now." Ms. Jones turned her attention to him.

Sidney smiled widely when Ms. Jones's sixth sense read his mind too. He could not believe it.

"Your comments were helpful because you shared openly what you thought when I asked how you perceived Kya's self-discipline. For many mothers, the comments you shared trigger a fight response because we all have a deep fear of being perceived as a bad mother."

With that landmine avoided, Ms. Jones said, "You two actually see Kya's self-discipline similarly. The good news here is that the district has prioritized creating strategies to support students with similar attributes to Kya, and it actively works with teachers to ensure the learning space does not unintentionally make students like Kya feel like something is wrong with them. We even have a parent education program to help parents like you understand the different research out there on ADHD, so you can make more informed choices consistent with your values. I can sign you up to receive that information now. Would you like that?"

"Yes, please," they replied, both letting out big sighs of relief.

It was 7:20 p.m. and Ms. Jones asked, "Do you have ten more minutes to complete the process?"

"Yes," they answered.

Feeling relieved, Mary grabbed Sidney's hand and gave him a warm smile. He returned it and gave her a quick kiss on the cheek.

As they jumped back into the questionnaire, they were both in agreement that Kya's resourcefulness was below where they thought it should be for her age, and they did not need to add any new insights for family supports and community resources since they had completed them for Chris's enrollment.

"Let's look at the Student Activity, Responsibility, and Emotional Profile section," continued Ms. Jones.

Mary pulled up the form. "At this stage," Mary said, "Kya doesn't have any activities that will consume her time. She will likely be involved in after-school sports or clubs, but we'll decide when school starts."

Sidney nodded in agreement. "She doesn't have any responsibilities like the ones you list in the survey."

"Does she have an IEP[20] or 504 plan[21]?" Ms. Jones asked.

"What's that?" asked Sidney.

"No," said Mary.

Ms. Jones answered, "I'll send you a link that will give you more information on IEPs and 504 plans, and the district's testing process and dates. Both the IEP and the 504 plan are given only after a child has been tested for needing special education resources or accommodations to support their learning. I think it would be good for both of you to review the information. If you have any questions, you can contact me. I'll make sure you get to the right person for answers or next steps."

"Thank you," Mary responded. "We'll review the information and get back to you if we have questions."

Sidney looked at the Emotional Profile section and said, "Kya took her birth parents' divorce really hard and has struggled with the idea of moving away from her biological father who lives in Los Angeles. She's very emotional about it. We're concerned and yet hopeful that things will get better with time."

"Thank you for sharing that information," answered Ms. Jones. "I'll make sure our team is aware and prepared to put our supports in place when school starts or even soon after you move, if that would be helpful."

"Now?" asked Mary in disbelief.

"Yes, now," Ms. Jones confirmed. "We believe it's important to help students as soon as possible when the need arises."

"Wow, let us give that some thought. Having supports in place right after we move could help ensure Kya gets off to a strong start at the beginning of the school year."

"Exactly," affirmed Ms. Jones. "I'll send you information on counseling support options for the summer, and you can follow up with me if you'd like to start before the school year begins."

"That sounds good," said Mary. "Thanks for that suggestion."

As Ms. Jones was scanning the notes, she saw Chris's emotional profile. "I'm looking at Chris's emotional profile now. Would you like to schedule an appointment with a student advocate to discuss support options for Chris as well?"

"That sounds like a good idea," agreed Sidney.

"Well," said Ms. Jones, "I believe we are all done for the evening since you have already shared how you'd like to stay informed and get engaged." She paused. "This will be in our email receipt, but you can expect to receive information on your assigned schools by the end of June. Once you find a house, please let us know the address so we can update our records and do our best to find the most appropriate school closest to your new home. Do you have any other questions this evening?"

"No," replied Mary and Sidney quickly.

"You're going to get a survey after our call asking how I did. I would surely be grateful if you would complete it. It's important for my supervisors and for me to know about your experience and what we can do to improve. We're really happy to have you joining us in Atlanta. It's been nice talking with you two. Y'all have a wonderful evening."

"Thank you so much, Ms. Jones. You were extremely helpful. We enjoyed talking with you." Mary's tone was warm with gratitude.

"You're welcome," said Ms. Jones. "Goodbye."

"Goodbye." Mary and Sidney both looked at the clock, which read 7:30 p.m., and then at each other.

"What just happened?" Mary said what they were both thinking.

"That was amazing," said Sidney. "In thirty minutes, we not only got Kya registered for school, but we got resources to learn more about supporting her learning and her transition to Atlanta, a referral to someone who can help us think through grief support for Chris, and coaching to help us avoid an argument we've frequently had."

They smiled at each other.

"Oh, before I forget," Mary exclaimed, "I'll make a note to call Chris's and Kya's schools tomorrow to ask for copies of their academic records."

Sidney nodded. "I'll check on the kids so we can get our family movie night started." Mary's wide smile made Sidney take one last sigh of relief before he jumped up to rally the kids.

Is this really possible?

Does this enrollment process excite you? If so, you may wonder why your district doesn't already have a process like this in place. Here are some common objections I've heard over the years and my responses to them.

What happens if an enrolling family doesn't have a permanent address at the time of preparing their enrollment application?

In many school systems, a family can only complete their enrollment application if they provide verification of a permanent address. One of the main reasons for requiring address verification is to ensure staff time and district funding go only to students and families in the district and school community they were intended to serve.

While some districts offer access to choice schools (which draws students from across their community) via a process with a later confirmation date, it's common for the enrollment experience to focus on identifying a school based on neighborhood. In both cases, the primary function of the enrollment process is to ensure that the number of students assigned to each school is clearly known and communicated to determine whether school budget projections are accurate or if staffing and resourcing modifications are necessary. The accuracy and transparency of school enrollment data during the budgeting process and the beginning of the school year is imperative, as it heavily influences what resources will be available to support students.

My intention here is twofold. First, it is *not* to say that focusing limited resources on students who will actually be attending the specific schools is wrong or unimportant. Rather, it's to state that there are other ways to achieve those same objectives without requiring an address to begin the process. Second, it is to say that requiring an address at the point of enrollment can cause relocating families to opt out of good public schools or choose the wrong school for their child.

What early insights about students in school systems are already captured, and why is more information necessary, particularly before the school year starts?

Many districts' enrollment applications focus on capturing a family's address and some foundational information, such as language spoken at home, child custody agreements, and whether the child lives with both parents. If a new student has previously qualified for special education (SPED), English Language Learners (ELL), or Highly Capable services in another school, the parent can often share that information during the process. That sharing adds a student to the appropriate program, but no action is taken before the school year starts. Instead, action is taken after the school year begins when the appropriate person can schedule time to assess whether the student qualifies for the program. The parent can only hope the central office programs' follow-up will happen in a timely manner when the school year begins and the school will have the supports their child needs. In other words, the student, teachers, and program are all starting from an information deficit about what the student may need to be successful at the beginning of the school year.

While this makes sense in the current system because funding for the student is tied to enrollment, this approach was not designed to be the best or quickest way to support the student's learning and development. It is also not optimal for setting teachers up for success in meeting students' learning and development needs. A considerable amount of instructional time can be lost or not fully maximized if a student does not have adequate supports available, such as special education, English language learner support, vision and auditory testing, connection to community partners to receive additional supports, etc.

While the enrollment process is already an impetus for assigning critical supports, such as language and special education services and student transportation, students' needs are becoming more specific. This means the notion that every teacher and staff person can be an expert on every student's needs seems unrealistic, unfair, and unsustainable. I believe this is one of the reasons why student outcomes data suggests that many students are in environments where they are not successful.

Having greater insights and awareness at the central office level could dramatically improve planning and resource allocation to better support students and teachers. For instance, because student needs are more specific, there are a number of central office departments (school community partnerships, family engagement, student services, and multi-tiered support programming) whose planning would benefit from early insights on students from families, former teachers, and students themselves. An approach that includes starting with parents' and students' needs and interests at the system level has the potential to create deeper connections between parents, teachers, students, community partners, and central office. Having these insights should be essential given the numbers of students struggling academically and socially and disconnecting from schools as well as the number of families facing barriers to staying engaged.

Won't parents be overwhelmed by the number of questions?

Parents always have the option to respond or not respond to questions, but I believe the potential for stronger partnerships between the school, district, community, and family to connect more resources to their child creates a compelling incentive for families to share their insights. I believe most parents would breathe a sigh of relief, realizing their district is this committed to their child's success, and will gladly take a few extra minutes to ensure their child gets better support.

What about data privacy? What will happen with all of this newly collected information?

Through the transformation process, school district communities would discuss data privacy and engage legal, policy, and technology experts to craft processes and policies that address their most common concerns. I am confident that thoughtful, intelligent minds can find a workable solution to data privacy that does not prevent students and families from getting the timely supports they need.

We're experiencing a budget shortfall and already have several priorities we haven't addressed. How could we afford a Ms. Jones and all the costs associated with making good on this new information?

Being concerned about the cost of new initiatives is understandable. However, to properly assess the potential cost, a structured analytical process will be necessary to compare the cost of inaction with the cost of a range of scenarios based on the shifts a district is willing to consider.

There is a real cost to systems *not* having an early and broad awareness of critical information that could enable central office departments to devise strategies and offerings to better support schools and students. These costs should be considered as options are weighed. There is also a cost when the needs of students and families do not coincide with the timing of when services are available. It's also important to remember the cost is not just financial. It shows up in low engagement and trust scores in organizational climate survey results, teacher and leader burnout, student and system outcomes, and overall stakeholder satisfaction results.

Transformation and the costs that go along with it do not occur at once or in a vacuum. It is possible for leaders to identify those costs and develop a bold, attainable, staged transformation plan tailored to their district's current realities, including making the most effective use of existing staff and community resources.

Are parent insights that valuable? What about the students whose parents may not be able to provide detailed insights? Would the benefit of this approach outweigh the cost?

In my opinion, it is essential to identify students' needs as early as possible so that program teams can provide them, their teachers, and their families with the necessary supports. Because parents are a child's first teachers, they often have good insights into their child's habits, motivations, and circumstances. While many teachers and counselors capture parent insights informally once the school year starts, these insights often stay at the classroom or school level, and if they stop there, central office leaders cannot identify the magnitude of the need. Consequently, they are not well-positioned to provide adequate supports or leverage community relationships to help school staff or students.

This approach would capture parent insights early and formally at the central level and involve training to help parents who may not feel equipped to provide detailed insights. If some parents were unable to provide this information, there are other approaches, such as having a family interview (student and parents) and preparing teachers to complete early assessments after getting to know the student. All in all, the benefits of this approach have the potential to outweigh the costs if it can reduce the number of students who need remediation or are at risk of dropping out.

A Deeper Look at How Data from Parents Can Make a Valuable Contribution to School System Planning

Parent Assessment of Students as Learners

As their child's first teacher, parents have unique insights into their child's tendencies, motivations, and approaches to learning. Understanding the parents' assessment of their child as a learner and a person should be a foundational element in a district-family partnership to help children reach their potential. The parents' insights, dreams, and aspirations (and their knowledge of their child's dreams and strengths) should help inform and influence central office resource planning and partnership formation. This information would give the school system an opportunity to plan more effectively, align resources to have the greatest impact on the most students, and explore school and teacher pairings that create the best fit and environment for success for everyone.

Student Activities, Responsibilities, and Emotional Profile

The student's activities, responsibilities, and emotional profile is about understanding each student as a unique person and enabling the school system to best meet their needs. As important as education is to a student's future, haven't we all encountered students whose after-school activities or responsibilities limit the time they have available to learn or access support? How about the student who has lost motivation because the traditional environment does not appeal to them, or their relationship with their teacher has deteriorated? Maybe they fell behind and don't know how they can catch up and have lost confidence, or are dealing with extreme anxiety. How many of us have witnessed students coping with a life shock such as a death, housing instability, or severe student anxiety, where learning has temporarily become a secondary or tertiary priority?

The schools' curriculum scope and sequence are outlined to cover a certain amount of content by the end of the year. This traditional school model impacts students differently based on their after-school interests and curiosities, family duties, and their learning, socio-emotional needs, and emotional profile. While teachers, counselors, etc., may do their best to help students catch up or keep pace, falling behind can be catastrophic and difficult for students to overcome. The data bears this out. Millions of students are not at grade level in core subjects and need learning environments that are more effective in helping them address their learning gaps, assuming the percentage of students performing at or above grade level reported in the Back Story[22] are representative across actual enrollment. Given the significant resources allocated to support students with different needs,[23] could we be more thoughtful in our delivery structure and design new pathways that not only meet students' needs but expand their opportunities to thrive?

In this way, the insights parents share on their child's activities, responsibilities, and emotional profile could help system staff provide better and faster supports to schools, students, and families. If the profiles are used effectively in system planning, it should be expected that profiles will be updated regularly by existing families, completed by new families, and supplemented with insights from school staff. Supplying families with a module in the student information system to update their child's profile throughout the calendar year, allowing important updates to be shared at any time (whether school is in session or not), can help school staff be better prepared to support a student immediately.

A district that is connected to and intentionally partnered with community organizations that address specific needs will find that an enrollment process similar to the one described above extremely useful. It will allow them to more effectively meet the ever-evolving needs of their students and alleviate unnecessary burdens from the teachers and school staff who have been trying to meet all of the needs without an effective process and system to support them.

With the insights provided by parents, the school and system staff should be in a position to work collaboratively to ensure students have the supports to remain and become independent, curious, joyful learners.

Helping Parents Stay Informed and Get Engaged

The Staying Informed and Getting Engaged questionnaire allows parents to customize the topics they receive updates about and the frequency with which they receive them.

While I have seen improvements in how some districts engage families, I have heard many parents say that they struggle to keep up with all the different opportunities to get involved and have missed many of them. As a parent, I am often overwhelmed by the frequent district emails, and I'm not confident that I will be able to stay informed of the decisions that are most important to me and my children. Plus, as a former school district executive, I can say that I have observed how a small-but-loud group of community members and family members can have a disproportionate impact because the districts did not have an efficient way for quickly polling all parents to get a representative perspective on key decisions.

It's vitally important to create a culture where parents and other stake-holders feel like valued and engaged partners helping to bring about a shared vision led by the board they've elected, the superintendent the board has hired, and the many staff who seek to support students, teachers, and families. Capturing parents' and other stakeholders' input and ensuring they are kept informed of important district decisions and other happenings go a long way to cultivating such a culture.

Why the Enrollment Experience Matters to Me

As a parent, I would have really appreciated an enrollment process like Phoenix County's when my family and I relocated from Denver to Seattle midyear in the early 2000s. My employer generously provided us with a house hunting trip before we moved to the city, during which we also began looking for schools. We had to find a preschool for our daughter to finish the school year and an elementary school in a strong feeder pattern into middle and high school. At the time, we were overwhelmed with all the options.

Even though it didn't address our immediate need for a preschool, we used the resources that were available at the time—national websites that allow parents to search for schools by test scores in particular geographic areas. My wife and I, having worked in and around K-12 education for many years, knew the limitations of this approach, but it was all we had. We narrowed our search to elementary schools rated "A" within ten miles of my employer and found ourselves looking at a list of fifty elementary schools with no additional way to narrow it according to our desires for our child.

Fortunately, my new employer also provided access to public and private school consultants to help us navigate this decision-making process. Several of my new colleagues were also happy to share their experiences as parents of young school-age children. When we talked to the private school consultant, she asked questions about our daughter's personality, dug deeper for what we were really looking for in a school, and then provided us with a list of three schools that met our criteria. We appreciated her in-depth sharing about the schools and their particular cultures and her thoughts about how our daughter would do in each one. Next up was the public school consultant, who told us that all the schools were good and we couldn't go wrong. It was good information, but we really wanted to learn about the school cultures and get a sense of how they would mesh with our daughter's personality and learning needs.

Our preference was a public school with some student diversity. We looked at the schools' demographics, student outcomes, mission and vision statements, and the student, teacher, and family responses to the school climate survey. This data helped us narrow our options to two schools that we decided to visit for an open house. At one of them, we loved the teacher who made an immediate connection with our daughter. We also appreciated the student diversity, which we later learned was due to an English Language Learner program that supported families who had immigrated from around the world. Just by chance, we discovered that the ELL program was moving to another school, which would dramatically decrease this school's student diversity. This change and some of the climate survey feedback gave us pause.

The other public school was a choice school that required an application process but didn't provide acceptance letters until after the deadline for the private school. Even though we felt it was the best option for our high-energy child of color, we weren't willing to take the risk that we wouldn't be accepted into the choice school. So we opted for the private school that had provided us with clearer answers to our questions and a clearer sense of their school community. When we learned a few weeks later that our daughter was admitted to the choice school, we were frustrated.

Since the public schools offered no tours, we couldn't see their school culture in action, and it was impossible to identify schools by the criteria that mattered to us. Plus, the decision calendars didn't line up, so we were forced to make bets on acceptance outcomes that did not seem reasonable, especially for folks new to the area.

When all was said and done, we were discouraged that we couldn't find the information (in a timely manner) we desired about the public schools in which we were interested. Unfortunately, this would not be the last time we felt our daughter's education and well-being were affected by school systems that did not make information available early enough for us to make the best decision for her.

In both cases, the schools we selected did not engage with us about our daughter and her needs and interests before we began the school year, and the follow-up throughout the school year did not meet our needs either. It did not appear that either school had considered the most common questions parents are likely to have or the possibility of preemptively addressing those questions in the orientation materials they shared and our initial interactions. This missed opportunity left us with choices for our daughter that were not aligned with our goals for her.

This was the outcome for two parents who know their way around education and school districts. We knew more going in, and we were still met with challenges at every turn. It is not difficult to imagine how many families and their students fall through the cracks to even greater degrees because they do not have equitable access to multiple learning environments, know what questions to ask, where to look for information they need, and how to advocate for their children's particular needs and interests.

As you will see throughout the rest of this book, asking for and organizing supports and resources around more insightful information on student needs and attributes before a child even sets foot in the school building is a powerful way to set them up for success (along with everyone responsible for their well-being and academic achievement).

Let's continue to explore a vision for how this data informs and improves school and central office planning and positively impacts student outcomes and the overall student and family experience.

Early the following week, Mr. Smith, a socio-emotional learning student advocate, opened his inbox and saw the enrollment forms for Chris and Kya. As part of a small team that receives the enrollment forms of all students who have experienced advanced trauma, his role is to ensure these students are placed in the optimal setting to support their healing and learning.

With a click, he opened the profiles and began reviewing the information.

I love my job, Mr. Smith thought. *Finding the right people, environments, and opportunities for each kid just… well, I wish someone had done this for me when I was a kid. I probably could have avoided a lot of disciplinary problems and lost instruction. And it would have made a huge difference for me supporting my own kids and some of the kids I coached on my basketball and soccer teams back in the day.*

Taking another sip of his coffee, Mr. Smith emailed Mary and Sidney. After explaining who he was and that he had reviewed Chris and Kya's enrollment forms, he asked if they would be available for a brief conversation so he could learn more and connect them with the right resources.

"Alright!" he said when his inbox dinged to show him that Mary had already responded and offered some times that would work. "Tomorrow at two o'clock it is!"

Reflection is a Key to Creating Your Own Personal Roadmap for Transformation

Set aside 45-60 minutes to journal. Reflect, write, review, repeat.

- What feelings emerged for you as read this chapter?

- What ideas sparked for your department or system?

- In your view, in what ways does leadership help or hinder the solutions coming to mind?

Download additional questions at www.EdImperative.org

73

Coordinating Supports to Meet Students' Needs

M r. Smith dialed the number for Mary and Sidney at the time they had set over email.

"Hello, Mrs. Wimbush. This is Mr. Smith from the Phoenix County school system. I'm following up to discuss the email I sent you and Mr. Wimbush."

"Hello, Mr. Smith. Thanks for calling. My husband is right here too." Mary signaled Sidney to join her at the dining room table as she put the social-emotional learning student advocate on speakerphone.

"Hello, Mr. Wimbush. It's nice to meet both of you. I know you must be busy preparing for your move, so I'll make this as quick as possible," Mr. Smith started. "I'd like to talk with you about some potential resources for Chris and Kya based on what I'm seeing in the enrollment questionnaire you completed."

"Sounds good. Where would you like to start?" Mary inquired.

"Let's start with Chris. I'd like to learn more about the support he's received since his mother passed and any changes you might have seen in his behavior since that time. I'd like to determine whether he would benefit from a rotation through our wellness center. The program is not for everyone, but it's designed to provide students dealing with a specific set of traumas, including traumatic grief, a space to support the healing process and their overall wellness. This is a self-contained specialty program that uses a variety of approaches to teach students coping and wellness strategies while giving them the space they need to begin the healing process. The district believes that the classroom setting may not be the best environment for some students who need additional care and attention. While participating in the wellness center, students receive small group tutoring and, where necessary, one-on-one tutoring to engage the content they missed at school and prepare them for their reentry into their assigned classrooms."

Sidney looked at Mary in amazement. He breathed a sigh of relief as he responded, "This is just what I was hoping for. Since his mother passed, Chris has withdrawn from us and most of his friend groups. His grades have dropped, and he seems lethargic—like he's just going through the motions. He has gone to a few counseling sessions but didn't develop a connection with the counselor. We've kept our eye on him, but we're very concerned. In fact, we're moving to Atlanta in part so Chris can be in more comfortable surroundings since he and his mother lived there before she passed. We also intend to find a counseling program after we relocate."

"I'm sorry to hear your son has been suffering. Based on what you've shared, I do believe that Chris would benefit from a rotation through the wellness center," Mr. Smith said as he noted his recommendations in the student advocate's note section of the student information system. "The school and teacher assignment teams will review my notes as they prepare Chris's schedule and make sure he's assigned a fall rotation through the wellness center."

The sounds of typing and clicking filled the brief silence before Mr. Smith continued.

"Okay, let's talk about Kya. Based on what you shared about her, I would like to suggest that Kya spend some time with the school counselor who will teach her the strategies they have compiled to support students dealing with their parents' separation or divorce. After the first couple of months of school, we can discuss her progress and any concerns you or the counselors may still have."

"That sounds like a good plan," Mary said, speaking for both of them.

"Wonderful. Well, I have what I need to start making these connections for your children. Do you have any questions or concerns I can answer?"

They looked at each other, both shaking their heads, and Sidney answered, "No, Mr. Smith. We really appreciate your help today. Thank you."

"My pleasure. Have a great day, you two, and please, always feel free to contact us if any questions or concerns do arise."

After they had all said their goodbyes, Mr. Smith completed his notes for Chris and Kya. Task accomplished, he sat back in his chair to enjoy the rewarding feeling of supporting children who are struggling, especially as it relates to the wellness center. For a long time, he was concerned that students experiencing acute trauma and childhood grief needed more support than many school counselors could give—more support than some children would ever receive.

Glancing at his calendar, he saw that it was almost time to begin the school and teacher assignment process.

Alright! Time for Ms. Clay and her team to work their magic!

A few weeks had passed since Ms. Clay had sat around the big conference table with the Multi-Tiered Support Services team, reviewing the student placements for the district's skill centers. These strategically located specialty centers provide personalized accelerated instruction from the district's top specialists to students who are a grade level or more behind in core skills.

As Ms. Clay scanned the roster, she saw Kya's name had been flagged, based on the early insight into Kya's learning needs from her parents, so she called Mary. "Hi, Mrs. Wimbush. I'm Ms. Clay, the Multi-Tiered Support Services team leader with the Phoenix County public schools. My team is responsible for connecting your children to the right support services and staff. I'm reviewing your assessment of Kya's academic skills, but I didn't see any previous records in the system. Do you have Kya's academic records—report cards or any available test results—so that we can better understand Kya's strengths and areas for improvement in her foundational skills? We recognize standardized assessments have limitations, but they will help us get an understanding of her skill levels."

Stunned at how proactive and responsive the district had been before her family had even moved to the city, Mary answered, "Thanks for following up. Since Kya's report cards and test scores have been packed already and are difficult for me to access, I requested copies from her current school. They just came this morning. I'll upload them before the end of the day."

"Great! Thank you. Let me know if I can be of further service between now and then," offered Ms. Clay.

"Thank you," Mary responded before saying goodbye and hanging up the phone.

That evening, as Mary uploaded the children's academic records and told Sidney about the call from Ms. Clay, his face brightened. "I'm growing more and more impressed by that school district."

The next morning, Ms. Clay immediately saw the update in her inbox, opened it, and reviewed Kya's past assessments.

Ah, yes. Kya is a great candidate for the skills center. She quickly picked up the phone and called Mary.

"Hello," Mary answered.

"Good morning, Mary. This is Ms. Clay from the Phoenix County School District. I received your email and Kya's information. Thank you for sending it. Based on what I'm seeing here, I'd like to talk more with you about our skills center. We believe Kya would make significant progress in our skills center and that it would set her up for success during the school year. I'd like to offer you two options. The first option is having Kya attend the summer program. This would strengthen her foundational skills in reading and math because we believe she has the potential to enter the new school year at grade level. Don't worry," Ms. Clay interjected quickly when she heard Mary take in a deep breath. "The summer skills program is interactive. Children play games. They move and have time outdoors. She'll love it. If the summer program doesn't work for your family, the second option is for Kya to join a skills center for a brief rotation in the fall after she becomes oriented at school." Ms. Clay went on to inform Mary that specialists at the skill centers are also experts in teaching students executive functioning, including the social executive functioning skills that are important as they make friends with peers and develop classroom success strategies.

As she described the skills center in more detail, Mary felt Kya would benefit from the opportunity immensely. "I think it would be great to have Kya attend the skills center over the summer so she can start the school year off strong," Mary responded happily. "Thank you so much for calling. I'm very impressed by your school system and how proactive everyone has been since receiving our enrollment form."

"I love this district for the same reason. We've come a long way in our journey to better support students and families," Ms. Clay affirmed as she logged her recommendations in the enrollment notes section of the student information system.

After Ms. Clay hung up the phone, her gaze fell on the Multi-Tiered Student Service (MTSS) deployment roster, which was a long list, organized by site, of students needing intervention supports and the intervention supports they would be receiving. She smiled, seeing that each school site and skills center had the experience and training mix they were striving for and that each school had the requisite skill and staffing to administer the district's MTSS strategy effectively.

If these supports had been available when Darren was struggling in school, I know his future would have been brighter. Ms. Clay said a quick prayer for her younger brother and went back to work, grateful that Kya and others had the opportunity to thrive despite their challenges.

Is this really possible?

Wouldn't the removal and reinsertion of students into wellness and skills centers disrupt the learning process, classroom management, and potentially students' self-esteem?

Not necessarily. With these supports, students have the opportunity to receive more direct, focused instruction tailored to their needs, which is the optimal scenario.

The reality is that many kids fall behind when they have skill deficiencies and their current classroom environment is not suited to help them overcome the issues and limitations they are facing, as evidenced by the data in the Nation's Report Card already shared.

I believe it is possible to intentionally design systems that, among other things, allow for specialists and teachers to stay aligned to:

1. ensure the skill center instruction helps students move forward in the general education curriculum;

2. support co-planning of instruction with a focus on helping teachers address differences in teaching style; and

3. demonstrate a One System, One School culture that recognizes and embraces that, at some point, students may have different needs and need to take additional steps to address them.

One System, One School Culture

A lot of systems use the right words, have solid strategies, and aspire to create healthy cultures, but the results aren't following. Why?

A One System, One School culture ensures every expectation, practice, process, program, subsystem, engagement, training, and decision is intentionally aligned and developed to effectively support students, families, teachers, and staff with helping their student(s) and team(s) achieve their individual and system learning and development goals.

With this new model, it will be essential to create a culture around the skills and wellness centers like the ones created around a physical therapy center, going to a dentist or doctor, or any skill-building training, such as learning a new language, instrument, or sport. The ethos around each of those offerings is that participation is essential to improving one's ability to function at desired levels, to be healthy, or to master a new skill. Within communities and districts, there needs to be an explicit effort to begin building personal and collective narratives that it is okay to start off with deficiencies in one's core academic skills, but it is unacceptable to not put forth the required effort to improve or to disparage someone who is trying to improve.

Wellness and skills centers, strategically located in the main regions of a school system, have the potential to provide students and teachers with a much-needed support system that allows both stakeholders to achieve individual and classroom goals. Ideally, the staffing strategy for those environments is designed to ensure that the professionals are exceptional at their craft and produce consistent results, making the process as effective as possible.

Is this an advanced form of tracking?

No. Historically, tracking meant low-income students and students of color would be put on a different, less-challenging curricular path, even when it wasn't a reflection of their needs or abilities. The skills centers would keep students on the same rigorous path as their class and provide additional support to close any skill gaps that inhibit their ability to perform at their best within that curriculum. Additionally, tracking carried with it social stigmas that would also be less likely to occur because at each phase of interaction with key processes and staff, this district is demonstrating a One System, One School formal and informal culture—a culture that recognizes and embraces that, at some point, students may have different needs and will need to take additional steps to address them.

The success of the skills centers is dependent on several achievable elements, including the execution of the mission, the effectiveness of the individuals hired, the coordination between the centers and the classrooms to which students return, resourcing, and the degree to which a prestigious and positive growth-minded culture surrounds it from both a teacher and student perspective.

Wouldn't the costs associated with the centers be prohibitive?

Not necessarily. School districts already spend significant dollars on interventions, remediation, and specialists aimed at supporting students. With fresh thinking and analysis, it's possible that undertaking skills centers could be achieved in part or in whole with existing resources.

Won't districts lose money if they're serving students before they have been admitted and counted in the district's funding formula?

Possibly, but not necessarily. There's a strong public policy interest in solving this problem because the student ultimately stays in the statewide community. Depending on the student need and resources available across the community, serving students better could simply be a matter of better coordination among agencies. In some cases, there may need to be intentional and coordinated effort to rethink program guidelines or advocate for such an approach. It's time to expand the services offered regionally so that school-age children are not prevented from receiving critical support services due to the timing in which their need arises (summer versus school year) or their uncertain living circumstances. It will certainly be important to incorporate controls so that costs don't skyrocket and super users do not consume more than their share, but this concern should not prevent creative thinking about how to make critical supports available year-round.

Why Getting the Right Supports in Place Matters to Me

As my daughter was nearing graduation from middle school, we began looking for a high school. Fortunately, the schools were offering student tours, and my daughter was able to get a good feel for each one. With her input, we chose a public school, enrolled in the early spring, and alerted the new school that she had a 504 plan.

It wasn't until the school year started—six months later—that we were told that the 504 plan from her private school would not be accepted. We were frustrated by this untimely communication and wondered why this information was not shared earlier—during the enrollment process or when we had submitted our information—so we could have taken the necessary steps to ensure she was supported for success from the beginning of the school year.

During the assessment meeting with her teachers a month or so into the first semester, they all told us she was progressing well. Due to COVID-19, the school had reduced the course load and relaxed some of the punitive consequences associated with late work, and they determined that, based on her early progress, she did not demonstrate a need for a 504 plan. While we were pleased with her progress, we were infuriated with the decision because we had several years of data points from her previous teachers, doctor, and a variety of learning specialists, and we knew the cycle of ups and downs that went along with being a student with ADHD and learning how to become an independent learner with stamina that lasts throughout the school year. We were told we could revisit the conversation if she had challenges keeping up when the school resumed in person with its six periods a day. We couldn't believe that she would have to demonstrate her struggle again in order to be given assistance, especially since many of the accommodations in her 504 plan did not cost any additional money. As it happened, she did struggle at the end of the year without being able to access the doctor recommended supports.

Unfortunately, when it came time to take timed tests for her classes, she didn't have the accommodation in place. Even with the Preliminary SAT (PSAT), we received no information from the school on how to navigate that process to ensure her accommodations would be recognized. As a parent, I felt unsatisfied because the information we needed was not easy to find, the school did not have a process for identifying or resolving these questions in a timely manner, and the standard for providing access to the 504 supports in the school did not feel aligned to what was in the best interest of our daughter.

Two years later, as she was beginning her junior year, we reached out to the school counselor to share the doctor's updated diagnosis, which outlined the types of accommodations she should have to support her learning. This time around, the school was extremely responsive. With essentially the same information we had before, minus feedback from her current teachers at the high school, accommodations were put in place at the beginning of the school year. This bypassed the typical process, which would have occurred a month or two into the school year. While we are very grateful these accommodations were made, my wife and I looked at each other with surprise, wondering why the same couldn't have been done two years earlier.

The room was buzzing with discussion as the group enjoyed a brief break when Superintendent Ellis entered. He took in the various conversations underway and noted the school assignment priorities posted on the wall and the notes hanging around the room. The school and teacher assignment teams were meeting, and it appeared they had already worked through returning students. Sitting around the room were all the student advocates, school leaders, school and teacher assignment leads who were directly involved in planning process. The dry-erase boards indicated there had been focused conversations about students and the environments that would best support their learning.

Ms. Johnston, executive director of student services, who was responsible for leading the school and teacher assignment processes, caught the superintendent's eye and walked across the room to speak with him. Her posture was open and friendly—a good match for her compassionate but in-charge personality. She had been working on this with the help of the mind-body practice she'd learned after receiving feedback from her team during the transformation process. Overall, she was feeling better than she had in decades, and it showed.

"Hello, Mr. Ellis," she started. "We're two-thirds of the way through the process, and we've had some rich, spirited discussions. So far, we've gone through our priorities list and feel confident that we've found placements that meet our standards for serving each student. Each will be in a school their family selected as one of their best learning environments, has an MTSS infrastructure well-suited to meet their needs, and is within our promised geographic range." She beamed as her eyes scanned the room full of specialized staff. "We haven't always agreed, but our mindfulness training has helped us stay focused on the task at hand and keep the tone of our conversations healthy and productive. I'm excited to do our after-action review to hear what others thought about the process and figure out what we can do better next year." She glanced at the wall clock. "Oh! Our break is over. I need to reconvene the group so we can stay on schedule. Was there anything in particular you wanted to know right now?"

Evan smiled back at her. "No, no. I was eager to see and hear how the new process is working. I appreciate you filling me in, and I look forward to learning more at our after-action review. Tell the team I said, 'Keep up the good work,'" he offered as he glided out of the room with a wide grin on his face.

Ms. Johnston turned her attention back to the task at hand. It was time to focus on students who needed to provide a home address. The leaders had a list of students with schools and, where appropriate, centers and teachers next to their names based on the match created by their profile from the enrollment form. Chris and Kya fell into this category of students without an address, and they were recommended for placement in the wellness and skills centers, respectively. The purpose of the conversation about these students was to go over the teacher assignments and to identify any partnership, staffing, and resource planning priorities that would need to be addressed to ensure a successful experience for the students, families, and staff.

There was a lively discussion about teacher assignments, including the strengths and profiles of the teachers and the needs of the students. The planning group felt confident that the teachers who either applied for, were nominated, or assigned to the wellness and skills centers had demonstrated their respective strengths and teaching style, and that the student enrollment form had elicited sufficient information to facilitate the matching process. The group was pleased by the enthusiastic emails they received from teachers who were selected to support these students after they completed their training and orientation program. As the meeting wrapped up, everyone was confident that teacher assignments had been informed by the best information available.

"Excellent work!" Ms. Johnston exclaimed. "I am very pleased with what we accomplished today and how the process worked this year, and there will be opportunities for you to share your feedback on the process and for us to dig into the parts that worked well and the areas that can improve. Please be candid in your feedback," she encouraged. "I also would like to thank Ms. Mendez and her recruitment team for recruiting so many new, excellent teachers so early in the recruiting cycle. It looks like their new recruiting strategies really paid off! Ms. Mendez, we are glad to have you back."

The whole room applauded Ms. Mendez, who had been noticeably quieter since returning from bereavement leave. Anyone who had spent any time with her knew she and her father had been very close, and they could see this loss had taken its toll. Ms. Mendez smiled warmly and expressed how grateful she was to be working in an organization that shows genuine concern for its colleagues.

Before adjourning, Ms. Johnston wanted the group to review the district's process for obtaining an address before final decisions were made on the fall school and teachers assignments. Satisfied that everyone was aware of the process and that parents would receive adequate communication to provide the necessary information before final decisions were made, she thanked the room full of enthusiastic student advocates and closed the meeting.

Is this really possible?

Does this approach eliminate parent choice and neighborhood schooling?

This vision necessitates changes in a couple of areas that some parents and school system leaders may view as untouchable. The simple answer is that this approach would use a community's priorities for the student experience and related outcomes as the basis for redefining what is meant by parent choice and neighborhood schooling. It would mean families aren't guaranteed a school; they are guaranteed an outcome—results in the school year, in a school within a certain radius from their home.

With this approach, districts have more flexibility to meet the unique needs of families clustered in micro-regions (a small group of bordering neighborhoods that are organized into a student support delivery zone).

Don't teacher assignments typically happen at the school level after enrollments are set? Doesn't this approach take important authority out of the hands of the school principal?

Like student assignment, this vision also necessitates changes in areas that may be considered off-limits. New and existing teachers would no longer be hired into a school or guaranteed a school. They would all work for the system and may be invited to change schools from time to time to best meet student needs. I believe if a system does an effective job of culture-building and establishing effective and repeatable processes for things like onboarding, educators should be able to rotate assignments and still build strong relationships with students and colleagues to meet the needs of the students.

Teachers would not be promised a school until the needs of the students across the district were considered in relation to the teachers' strengths. While these criteria would need to be negotiated through a collective bargaining process, the vision is that teachers would be promised employment within a specified radius of their home and would be assigned based on their strengths, interests, and the district's needs. The district would offer a range of options to identify and incentivize teachers to take on high-priority assignments. Without question, many details would need to be worked out, including processes that provide appropriate transparency and opportunity for input by school-level leaders, but such an approach holds the possibility of creating better learning environments and outcomes for students and teachers.

What is this new role of student advocate, and can we afford it?

The student advocate's role is to understand the needs of the students in their caseload and serve as a safety valve to ensure the students are receiving the classroom, school, central office, and community supports they need to thrive. Having worked in large school districts for many years, I believe this role is vital. It's common for leaders to talk about programs and services as proxies for students because the students are too many to name. While this is an understandable approach, it often unintentionally depersonalizes the system because students' stories and needs get lost in efforts to communicate about programs and services at an aggregate level. Often the assumption is that the program addresses all of the students' needs, but that is not always the case. By creating the student advocate role, the student is reinserted into the conversations that take place within planning meetings, and their unique needs are represented in a manner that is much more personalized and prevents the need for proxy references.

As to whether a school system or community can afford student advocates, that question can best be answered after an analysis of the staff and financial resources available in the school system and broader community. A comprehensive understanding of both should yield a range of potential options.

What is mindfulness, and how does it support this new approach?

The learning environment is more than an academic space. It is a rich mixture of the cultures and life experiences of all of the stakeholders—students, teachers, parents, partners, school and central office staff, and others. The life experiences that shape the learning environment include not only the educational training and positive experiences individuals bring but also their traumas, difficulties, and biases. Unfortunately, it is common for these traumas and biases to play out in the learning environment. Words, actions, and even activities may unconsciously activate an adult or student, creating a learning environment that doesn't always feel safe or welcoming. These traumas can also make it impossible for district staff and community members to have the hard conversations necessary to move a system forward.

"Mindfulness," as Dr. Niki Elliott states, "is the practice of focusing on being intensely aware of what one is sensing and feeling in the moment, with a lens of acceptance and nonjudgment. The experience of being mindful gives individuals the ability to have full attention to present moment awareness and the ability to create enough space between themselves and their unconscious thought patterns to allow something new to emerge. This new thing may be a creative insight, a sense of peace, a resolution to a pressing problem, or simply an expanded awareness of self or another. Mindfulness strategies include breathing methods, meditation, affirmative visualization, and other practices that relax the body and mind, help reduce stress, and increase social engagement and collaboration."[24]

Interpersonal neurobiology is demonstrating that self-regulated leaders are more resilient, capable of accessing their higher-order thinking and problem-solving abilities, and adept in building healing-centered relationships. I believe having leaders with these skills is critical for insulating against burnout and turnover as well as restoring and strengthening trust within community relationships, creating a healthier school and community culture, and dramatically improving student outcomes.

Personal and collective mindfulness practices have the potential to accelerate the efforts of district leaders and staff to transform their educational systems from their boardrooms to their classrooms.

The following week, Ms. Johnston scanned her notes from meetings with the school community partnerships, multi-tiered support services, school assignment, and teacher assignment teams. Her next task was to summarize the resources she would need to advocate for in order to ensure the school and central office staff and community partners would have the resources they needed to support students and families by addressing the priorities they shared during their enrollment process. Ms. Johnston also knew where she would need to work with the superintendent and grants team to seek additional funding to enhance specific community partnerships that support students as well as offer additional professional development to teachers in the wellness and skills centers.

I've got my work cut out for me, but I know the planning these leaders do to allocate and attract new resources to meet students' needs is far more advanced than the last district I worked in, Ms. Johnston thought.

Later that afternoon, Ms. Clay, Ms. Johnston, and Mr. Smith huddled in an informal staff meetup in the central office atrium and talked quietly, despite their excitement.

"In my twenty years in this school system," said Mr. Smith, "I have never seen such an intense focus and coordination to support students, school teams, and families. We're more integrated and aligned than we've ever been! Our system makes more sense now. I believe our students, families, and school and central staff agree. The changes we've made have really taken our efforts to better support every student and family to the next level."

The two ladies smiled broadly in agreement and then went back to work sorting out the final details.

Following the school and teacher assignment processes, the enrollment team sent a letter to families letting them know their assigned school and wellness and skill center placements and reminding them of the deadlines for providing missing information that could change their assignment. The letter also reminded families of the agreements they made at the beginning of the process, which included an acknowledgment that changes after the agreed-upon deadline would put the early and additional supports at risk and limit personalization, as changes after the deadline would significantly increase costs.

Mary and Sidney received the enrollment letter with Chris's and Kya's school assignments and tentative teachers for the fall. When Mary opened the letter and began reading it, she saw the deadline for letting the district know their new home address and shared that information with her husband.

"I believe we'll have a new home by then," Sidney said with optimism.

"I'm really glad to have this process taken care of *before* our move," Mary mused as she put a note up on the family's to-do list.

"I agree. It's a huge relief."

Reflection is a Key to Creating Your Own Personal Roadmap for Transformation

Set aside 45-60 minutes to journal. Reflect, write, review, repeat.

- What feelings emerged for you as read this chapter?

- What ideas sparked for your department or system?

- In your view, in what ways does leadership help or hinder the solutions coming to mind?

Download additional questions at www.EdImperative.org

Aligning Supports to Meet Students' Needs

M r. Garcia, executive director of the Learning Options portfolio, was reviewing his schedule when he noticed it was time for the report on the central office budget planning priorities to be posted. Opening up a spreadsheet, he began reviewing the critical resource needs that surfaced during the school improvement planning process, student enrollment and assignment process, and the central office budget planning conversations. He printed the file, picked up his notebook, and left his office.

As he strolled into the auditorium with his usual energy and enthusiasm, he greeted colleagues from across the central office. Noticing that Ms. Johnston had a seat open next to her, he greeted her. "Hello, Ms. Johnston. Is anyone sitting here?" When she smiled and replied that it was available, he sat down and opened his notebook.

"I'm eager to hear the results of the prioritization process," he said, looking relaxed in his chair. "It's a big change from last year. I felt like it wasn't clear how trade-offs between competing budget needs were decided, and whether important needs even made it into the prioritization conversation at all."

"I agree," said Ms. Johnston. "Nevertheless, I'm still a little nervous that some of our important funding needs will not be met."

Evan and his cabinet leadership team walked into the room together, nodding and greeting staff as they took their seats at the head of the auditorium.

Evan addressed the group. "Thank you all for your time and efforts to support our students and our future. I realize many of you may be anxious about the results of the process, and I want to assure you that we are committed to supporting you in finding the resources required to meet the needs of our students, staff, and families…"

He gave a high-level overview of the planning process—the time-line, and school, central office, and partner planning processes—that were used to inform the priorities list. Then he walked through the items that were prioritized for funding by department, discussed the items that would be prioritized for grant funding, and explained the decisions for not prioritizing specific items.

Why Budget Planning Matters to Me

Early in my career, I was hired as a consultant to help a school district committed to becoming a world-class school system develop a five-year strategic financial plan to support their efforts. Rather than ask leaders to make a wish list of all the things they would do if they had additional resources, I wanted to understand what the respective program teams were trying to accomplish with the annual funding they requested and use those insights to inform multiyear planning. I created a planning process with templates and training to go along with them.

My process for understanding annual budget needs was very different, requiring more thought (and time) than the incremental budget process they were accustomed to using. In their incremental budget process, the program managers would input the amounts of resources they were requesting beyond the funding they received the previous year and provide a sentence explaining the purpose of the additional funding. The budget team would compile all the budget requests and present them by department and division. In my observation, the one-sentence rationale for the funding was dropped from the financial summaries shared by finance. In the end, the qualitative rationales supporting the funding requests were not presented in a structured way, which limited objective prioritization.

I wanted to understand, among other things, what service delivery promises and performance metrics they were trying to achieve with the additional funding *and* the impact of not doing anything. These insights would position leadership to have necessary strategic, tactical, and philosophical conversations internally. They would also help manage stakeholder expectations if funding was not secured. When budget managers completed their forms, I would review them and meet with the managers to help them clarify and refine their submissions so their funding goals were clear before they were shared.

A couple of the comments from my interviews have stuck with me through the years.

One longtime program manager said, "In my thirty years in the district, no one from finance has *ever* asked me what resources I need to do my job more effectively." In this particular instance, the program manager was requesting funding to fulfill the district's promise of equitable distribution of music equipment to all kids.

When I sat down with another program manager to help her determine if her planning form was capturing the main needs of her program's stakeholders, she said, "You know, as I think about it, when we develop our teacher professional development budget, it often meets our training needs for teachers who start at the beginning of the year, but we're out of money for training new teachers who are hired in January."

Circumstances changed, and the district did not complete the five-year strategic financial plan we set out to develop. But even this nascent work I had done with the program manager had made a difference.

Months later, while I was wrapping up work on a different project within the district, I heard someone calling my name as I entered the building. When I turned around and saw one of the program managers I had interviewed, she greeted me and got straight to her point. "I was skeptical of your process. But the other day when my boss called me to ask me for information on my program, because of your process, I had the information ready for her, and I got the funding I was hoping for!"

When I reflect on my school district experiences and observations as a consultant, the large urban districts I have examined (at least according to their budget calendars) did not have an adequate, structured budget planning process. An effective, structured budget planning process digs into what teams are trying to accomplish and integrates insights from annual central office department and school planning processes to develop a comprehensive list of operational and strategic budget requests for prioritization. Such a process is necessary to ensure leaders do not lose sight of important priorities that require funding. It also helps eliminate funding of strategies in a piecemeal fashion at inadequate levels across departments.

Given limited district resources, inevitably there will be departments that do not receive the funding they need or believe they need to be successful. However, having a process that helps leaders make a clear, well-conceived case for funding is essential for strengthening the budget prioritization and resource allocation process and communicating the system's goals and objectives to the public. It is also imperative for districts to have an appeals process in case important information was overlooked or misunderstood, as well as a development team focused on securing grant dollars to fund exploratory work, scale, demonstration sites, planning grants, etc., for which resources may not be available in a given budget year. Even with adequate planning, it is not always possible to identify and secure grant funding within one's annual planning calendar. When grant, partner, general, and capital funds are not available to support a priority, it is vital there be clear communication about what was not funded and what that means for that body of work for the coming year and beyond. Too often, work is inadequately funded, expectations are not managed, and stakeholders often believe the same scope, schedule, and outcomes are possible, even though the work was not fully funded. This misperception creates and compounds mistrust and frustration across communities and relationships.

When I joined a large urban school system as deputy superintendent, I inherited a district that had gone through five years of budget cuts totaling $115 million, resulting in major changes to programs and services. I used the budget planning process referenced above and embedded it within another process referred to as the Service Improvement Cycle. The Service Improvement Cycle started with a school leader satisfaction survey covering central service department's customer service, processes, and training programs. Then we conducted focus groups to unpack the challenges that were driving the perceptions of the departments with the lowest satisfaction ratings. The departments used the focus group feedback to further explore and develop action plans aimed at addressing the identified needs. The target completion of the action plans flowed into the budget development process and created the detail necessary to support a robust review and prioritization process. To be clear, not everyone was always happy with the outcomes, but the transparent process went a long way toward building trust within the system and improving our ability to ensure limited resources were reaching the areas we prioritized at the appropriate time.

Ms. Johnston looked over at Mr. Garcia and said, "Well, we didn't get funding for everything we needed, but I am pleased with the items that have been prioritized and the commitment to pursue funding for others. I appreciate that they helped us see the big picture so we're better able to support their decisions. Makes the disappointment a little easier to swallow. What did you think?"

Mr. Garcia's stoic stare turned into a furrowed brow. "I don't get it," he started. "We say we want to give teachers an opportunity to create new learning environments for our students so that it's not only outside organizations offering new options within our district, but we don't provide nearly enough funding to support our teachers with making the transition. It's really frustrating!" His tone was low but emphatic. "We have nearly a dozen internal teams that are launching new school offerings in response to the student and parent survey and, in my view, the available funding won't be enough for them to adequately plan before school opens."

"I'm sorry to hear that," replied Ms. Johnston, noticing his typical can-do attitude evaporating. "Will you use the appeals process the superintendent referenced to share your concerns? In my experience, the leadership team has been accessible and open to receiving feedback and listening to concerns."

Taking a deep breath, gathering himself, and reflecting on Ms. Johnston's question, he responded, "That's my experience too. It's a good idea. I'll use that process."

After saying his goodbyes, Mr. Garcia went back to his office and forwarded the superintendent's communication on priorities and the appeals process to the Learning Options Volunteer Advisory Task Force, which was composed of parents and community leaders. They had a meeting scheduled that evening in anticipation of discussing next steps after the superintendent announced his initial budget priorities, and Mr. Garcia had a lot of work to do to build a stronger case for funding during the appeals process.

When it was time for their brief check-in meeting that evening, Mr. Garcia was ready. He began the virtual meeting by welcoming each volunteer in turn as they logged on.

Mr. Kahn, a parent member of the task force, took the lead. "Thank you for sharing the budget priorities and appeals process with us, Mr. Garcia. I had a chance to talk briefly with the parents this afternoon. We've all read the materials and want to know how we can support you in the appeals process. Oh, and we also have a prospective task force parent joining us, Mary Wimbush. She's relocating from LA with her husband and two kids."

Mr. Garcia smiled widely. "I appreciate you all touching base prior to our meeting so we can make the most of our limited time. And thank you for joining us today, Mrs. Wimbush. Let me share my screen briefly so everyone can see the narrative I've prepared for the appeals application."

After reviewing the brief document, the members gave feedback they thought would help strengthen the case for the appeal. They were fortunate to have a wide range of experiences on the task force, including recent immigrants who participated with the support of their high schooler, parents who work two jobs and could only meet in the evenings, and parents who had backgrounds in marketing, budgeting, and training.

Realizing their forty-five-minute meeting was nearing an end, Mr. Garcia summarized the main takeaways he'd heard from the parents, reaffirmed his intention to appeal, shared when he expected he'd be able to provide the task force with an update, and thanked everyone for their creativity and time.

After logging off from the meeting, Mary was exhilarated. She immediately went upstairs to where Sidney was watching the basketball game.

"Hey, honey. Would you pause your game for a second? I've got to tell you about the Learning Options Task Force meeting I just participated in. The task force learned today that the department won't be receiving the funding they hoped to receive, and they were discussing a draft of the appeals application Mr. Garcia, the head of the Learning Options portfolio team, planned to submit.

I was really impressed with the way the group came together. It would have been easy for them to be upset or feel the need to fire off emails complaining to board members, but they didn't do that. They really tried to understand if the funding they didn't receive was necessary and how to make sure their needs were clearly communicated in the appeal process."

"That's great." Sidney beamed. "When will you find out if the task force's efforts helped attract the additional dollars?"

"In a week," Mary replied. "But even if the Learning Options portfolio doesn't get additional funding in the proposed budget, we are hopeful the superintendent will be committed to helping the team find additional resources."

The next day, Mr. Garcia submitted a request for an appeal.

A few days later, he met with the budget director, the chief financial officer, the chief academic officer, and the superintendent. He expressed his and the task force's concern and shared new information on the composition of the internal teams that had been approved to open new schools. He also made his case for funding to support the development of a new competency-driven school for the Learning Options portfolio so that students were not tied to the traditional classroom-based learning hours.

Based on the new information shared, the team believed Mr. Garcia's request warranted funding support, and the superintendent tasked the CFO with finding the additional funding. When Mr. Garcia emailed the update to the task force, he was surprised to see the stream of celebratory emails within the hour. As he sat back in his chair, a relaxed smile crossed his face.

I'm grateful to have the parent task force. Our check-in conversation really helped me sharpen my focus so I could frame the resource needs more clearly in the appeal. I know it's what made the difference. Now we have the resources we need to implement the plan we designed.

With the funding conversations completed, Ms. Johnston and Mr. Garcia were excited to dig into the findings from the master schedule audit. The insights from the findings would be essential to creating the time necessary for teachers to work more collaboratively, learn from one another, and strengthen their plans to support students.

Mr. Garcia walked into a small conference room where three individuals were already seated and waiting for him.

"Hello, Ms. Williamson, Ms. Johnston, Mr. Jolly." He greeted them with a bright smile.

After a few mutual pleasantries, Mr. Garcia officially began the meeting. "Thank you for your willingness to participate in this planning meeting to determine how to best share the findings from the master schedule audit with school leaders. I believe the insights from the audit will also help us find common spaces for professional development across the district. These spaces will make it easier for teachers to learn from one another by grade level and subject expertise as well as co-plan ways to ensure students rotating through the wellness and skills centers stay connected to their home school communities."

The others nodded in agreement.

"I'm excited that we're finally able to have this conversation," added Ms. Jolly, the district's chief academic officer. "In my fifteen years in the district, master schedules stayed at the school level. We've never had a districtwide process to help us learn from each other. This is a game-changer," she said in her typical matter-of-fact, no-nonsense tone. "It took me a long time to figure out how to be the master of the schedule. This initiative is long overdue."

Ms. Williamson, master schedules process director, chimed in before bringing the focus back. "We have such great instructional leaders in the district. I believe there's a lot to learn from one another. Since this will be our first discussion of the master schedule audit, I think it's important to explain the decisions that need to be made, gain agreement around the student- and teacher-focused objectives we all want to achieve, and be clear about which ones will be school, joint, and central decisions."

"I agree," said Ms. Jolly. "It'll be important for everyone to see and understand that our student support system requires greater scheduling coordination to facilitate common and unique teacher professional development and student transitions between the skills and wellness centers and their home schools."

"And let's not forget our community partners," said Ms. Johnston, her expression focused but pleasant. "Some of them will be providing tutoring and other support to our students. To the extent they are available, they should be invited and encouraged to participate in our teacher training to ensure students are not confused by the different approaches."

"Well said," Mr. Garcia remarked as he handed out a draft annotated agenda for the meeting with the school leaders for the group to review, discuss, and refine.

At the end of the meeting, Mr. Garcia recapped the changes to the agenda, the discussion points they agreed were important, individual roles in the meeting, and the materials that should be sent in advance.

"I think we've got a good plan," he said confidently as he closed his notebook and looked into the faces of his purpose-driven peers.

The others nodded in agreement and said their goodbyes.

That afternoon, Mr. Garcia sent an email update to the Learning Options Task Force. He shared his excitement about the findings of the master schedule audit, the upcoming conversation with school leaders, and what could be possible for students and teachers as a result of insights from the audit. He drew a connection between the task force's work and support of the budget that made the audit possible.

Mary smiled as she read Mr. Garcia's email, feeling a deep sense of inspiration and gratitude for having attended that meeting.

I really appreciate how they enabled me to get involved so quickly, even though my kids haven't officially started school in the district. Mary signed out of her email. *I'm so glad they met virtually and had a process that enabled me to get the context of the conversation prior to the call so I could be informed and in a position to contribute.*

Later that day, Ms. Johnston joined the school community partnership team for a planning meeting.

"Welcome, Ms. Johnston." Mr. Kim, the school community partnerships director, greeted her in his typical stoic-but-kind fashion and gestured toward the open seat and the meeting agenda placed in front of it. "I just finished sharing a bit of our department's history and how our mission has been expanded to better align our partnerships with the district's multi-tiered support services and career readiness strategies."

"Yes," Ms. Johnston replied as she scanned the room. Seeing a few new faces, she decided to emphasize a couple of key points she was confident Mr. Kim had already shared. "We weren't always known as a good partner, but when our board and district leadership took the next step in our efforts to deepen our impact with students, we recognized that several of our community partners bring expertise that is critical to our students' success. We've committed to working more closely with our community partners to support our shared students, which includes inviting them to participate in our planning and professional development meetings. It's imperative that we make it easier for students and families to connect to essential support services, enrichment, and other activities that inspire them, as well as internships and other opportunities to prepare them for life after high school."

"That's right," affirmed Mr. Kim when Ms. Johnston gestured for him to take over. "Over the last several weeks, we've been reviewing the findings from each school's gap analysis between the community partnership offerings and the needs identified in the students' activities, responsibilities, and emotional profiles. We also reviewed the student satisfaction surveys and partner outcomes data as well as the partner survey feedback that examines school collaboration and coordination. You'll see that we've converted that data into a red, yellow, green status report for each school with respect to their school community partnerships."

When he handed Ms. Johnston a copy, she smiled at the sea of green. However, as she scanned the page, her brow furrowed as she more closely scrutinized the handful of schools whose status was either red or yellow.

"We were just planning to discuss the status report, specifically those items that have been identified as warranting escalation, needing school resolution, and requiring community partner conversation," continued Mr. Kim when he noted her expression.

"Great!" said Ms. Johnston, shifting her perspective from concern to curiosity as she opened her computer and leaned back in her chair to listen. "Please proceed."

At the end of the hour, Ms. Johnston had developed a good sense of the conversations she needed to have with the stakeholders targeted in her team's status update. She would talk with local funders about the availability of resources to support the work of community partners in the schools. A talk with the superintendent and board would be necessary to give them a heads-up on community partners' performance that warrants improvement before continuing. Plus a call with the chief of schools would catalyze the development of a strategy for supporting a few schools whose partners were struggling to engage. She also had a good sense of what her team needed to accomplish to support the remaining schools in putting partners in place to fully engage students at the beginning of the school year.

As she stood up from her seat, Ms. Johnston acknowledged her team with a genuine smile. "Nice work, you all! Our division summary for the first release of the Opening of School Report is due in two weeks. With the steps you've outlined, I believe we're on track to have a strong start to the school year."

Their authentic expressions of happiness were conveyed before she made her way to the door.

Why Partnerships Matter to Me

When I became deputy superintendent, I initiated an effort to reposition our school community partnership department from one that primarily established data-sharing agreements to provide partners with student data that would help them better support the students they served to one that aligned community partners to provide the wraparound supports schools did not have staff or capacity to provide.

Initially, this process was met with some resistance and hesitancy at the central office level. Some leaders declined to invite community partner organizations to key trainings as they understandably believed their primary and sole role was to provide training for district employees, not for community partners. It also took time to engage other leaders and community partners because of the negative experiences they'd had when working together previously.

After several meetings (both individually and collectively), our district leadership and school community partnership team made some meaningful progress building rapport, trust, and readiness for this new approach. Two partnerships stand out. One was with our city's department of education and early learning, which had its own levy funding to implement a variety of school improvement and intervention strategies. The other was our local housing authority, which housed 12 percent of the district's student population.

Through these partnerships and others, the district took significant strides forward in making sure our district and community partners were working in a more coordinated manner to serve our students with the highest needs.

Later that week, Ms. Johnston joined a virtual meeting with Mr. Talladesse, the student advisor support manager. The purpose of their meeting was to debrief lessons learned from the current school year, discuss some of the changes that would be made to the student advisory supports in the coming school year based on their planning requests, and thank the student advisor leads for their work as the school year was coming to a close.

"Greetings, Mr. Talladesse!" Hello, Mr. Talladesse! Hey, Mr. Talladesse, said various members of the group when his face appeared on-screen. Everyone present appreciated the positivity and energy he brought to their workplace, even when it was virtual.

"Hello, team!" After briefly posing an informal check-in question to connect with the group, Mr. Talladesse said, "We have a full agenda this afternoon. So, let's get to it! A copy of the agenda was attached to the meeting invitation, and it's also on the screen for your review. First, I want to thank you for encouraging your students and advisors to complete their end-of-year feedback forms. Each of your schools received rich responses. There were many positive responses about the increased time available for student advisories in the school schedule. There were also some good suggestions for improvement. We're looking forward to sharing this districtwide summary with you and working together to chart a path forward."

Switching screens, he continued. "Your peers on the student advisories steering committee have developed a series of questions to help inform how to best use the survey information. I've dropped a link in the chat box that will take you to the form where you can type your responses. They will guide the steering committee in refining the program next school year.

The advisors spent the next several minutes reflecting on the feedback and responding to the prompts. Their responses came streaming in.

When he saw the final one, Mr. Talladesse thanked everyone. "Excellent! Thank you for your insights and ideas! Let's take five minutes so you can review each other's responses. Please add any additional ideas you have if reviewing others' responses stimulates new thoughts."

After five minutes, Mr. Talladesse brought that part of the meeting to a close. "Thank you for sharing your ideas. The steering committee will follow up with you again when they have a draft set of program improvements recommendations to share with you."

Stopping the screen share, he shifted gears. "Now, I have some good news to share. The two requests we made during the budget planning process were successful. The additional funding will allow us to procure the new advisory curriculum and advisor training support that you all recommended. Additional funding will also allow each of your schools to have a modest budget to increase the range of staff to support your school advisory program." His announcement elicited big smiles from everyone. When he was finished with his comments, Mr. Talladesse invited Ms. Johnston to say a few words before he adjourned the meeting.

"Thank you, Mr. Talladesse. Good afternoon, everyone," said Ms. Johnston. "I wanted you to know that the superintendent expressed enthusiasm for this work because he also sees it as critical to supporting students' socio-emotional well-being and their academic success." She went on to thank the student advisor leads for their leadership throughout the school year and their colleagues for all they did to support students and one another. Finally, she extended her gratitude to the student advisory steering committee, a newly formed group created to help elevate teachers' voices in the central office planning and implementation process.

As Mr. Talladesse and Ms. Johnston talked, clapping and thumbs-up emojis flooded the screen.

"I hope you all enjoy a great close to the school year," offered Ms. Johnston before the meeting ended.

A few weeks later, Ms. Johnston sat at her desk reviewing the Student Service Alignment Exceptions Report, which highlights students by school who may not have the right complement of supports (based on their enrollment submission and feedback from one or more of the following individuals: student advocate, community partner, counselor, or teacher in the student information system). She was scheduled to meet the student advocates later that day and wanted to make sure they felt empowered and prepared to address each of the outstanding issues in front of them.

As Ms. Johnston perused the list, she noticed that while the percentage of students on the report was small compared to the total student population, there were still quite a few students on it. She studied the report and notes provided by the student advocates for nearly an hour and looked at the numbers and behind the numbers for trends, questions, and answers. The advocates' notes summarized a path forward to resolving each student's needs. They were organized by issues that required escalation to Ms. Johnston or peer departments, outreach to colleagues in peer departments, and clarification from parents or a member of students' support teams (teacher, counselor, community partner, etc.). She made a list of questions for each advocate, and later that day, she was pleased to see that each advocate came prepared to discuss all the questions she had about items flagged for escalation.

By the end of the meeting, Ms. Johnston had a good handle on the barriers facing the students whose support plan had been escalated to her. She also felt confident that the student advocates had a clear understanding of what they needed to get done before the end of June to ensure that all partners had the best information to plan for the students' arrival on the first day of the school year.

"Nice work, everyone!" Ms. Johnston said. "I'll look forward to seeing your progress in the student information system and discussing it during our next check-in. If you need me for anything in the meantime, please be sure to reach out."

Is this really possible?

The master schedule audit sounds intriguing, but we have provisions in our collective bargaining agreements that will make implementing any recommendations difficult.

The unions play a vital role in the schools and could play a vital role in the learning process that the master schedule audit enables. Specifically, the problems that the master schedule audit is designed to speak to are many of the top reasons educators frequently cite for leaving the profession, such as the desire for greater collaboration with colleagues in the same department and similar roles in other schools; working conditions that don't feel so chaotic; disjointed professional development; deeper impact in their realm of influence; and more professional development during the work day instead of evenings and weekends.

In addition to yielding valuable insights that will improve instruction and professional development opportunities for educators, depending on the design of the audit, it can also reveal opportunities to better support students and the learning environment in key areas such as transportation, food services, athletics, etc.

Many districts use an interest-based bargaining process,[25] a method for helping two sides to reach agreement by trying to find ways in which both sides can get what they want. This approach is effective but very incremental and is not driving us quickly enough toward the outcomes or work environments we desire. We need a space in communities where union leaders and district leaders can engage more freely in a creative exploratory process to discover what big transformative change is possible in the near term based on their shared priorities. Such a process could be a parallel process that allows a small group of district and union leaders to explore what it would look like to work collaboratively from scratch (or take bigger chunks of programs/services) and be more imaginative about how to redesign the system, so it works better for all parties involved. Such an exploratory approach should not be considered binding until a commitment to execute is made.

We believe in partnerships, but we've been burned by them too. Are partnerships really worth the trouble?

In my view, community partnerships provide a significant opportunity to fundamentally improve the delivery of services to students and families, reducing the friction they often experience in accessing those services. For that reason alone, it should be an imperative that school districts and community organizations take bolder action to improve, deepen, and maintain continuous alignment of interests within their partnerships.

True, many factors can cause a partnership to be ineffective and difficult to terminate or restructure. However, there are many proven ways to mitigate those risks and address those realities.

The shared objective to see students thrive should make leveraging partnerships to achieve deeper impact a very attractive strategy.

We already have so many meetings in our school district. This approach just seems to add more to our schedules. Why is this considered a good thing?

The proposed approach focuses on designing interactions that organize stakeholders around meeting specific student needs in the flow of planning and delivering services. In my experience, when a thoughtfully-designed structure is not in place, issues rise from the school to the central office in a piecemeal manner, which can be overwhelming to manage. This ad hoc approach doesn't foster systemic problem-solving. For this reason, I believe an intentional meeting structure is necessary and will be more effective and efficient because it should result in fewer piecemeal meetings and lead to sustainable systemic changes.

Don't all these centralized processes take authority away from the schools?

They shouldn't. If done correctly, these processes should empower schools by demonstrating the dialogue and action that are informed at all levels with their ideas and participation. In my experience, there is a critical service gap between the schools and central office. It's not uncommon for schools to exhaust their ability to meet some students' needs in the building long before there is central office support, if support is available at all. These proposed new processes are aimed at helping central offices dramatically improve their ability to leverage their districtwide insights and role in the community to foster partnerships and offerings that close the service gap between the school and the community.

Ms. Mendez, chief of human resources, sat in her office reviewing the recruitment status report that highlighted the number of vacant positions, offers made, and interview dates, among other things. After studying the status report to get a sense of whether the recruitment team was on track to complete its school-based hiring before the end of the school year, she realized there was nothing in the report that required an immediate follow-up. The team had good plans underway for each open position.

After participating in the teacher assignment process, she felt very comfortable that the recruiters had a good sense of what skill sets and attributes they needed to find for the remaining open positions and the compensation necessary to be competitive.

This looks like we have the potential for a great recruiting year! Ms. Mendez thought.

After adding a couple of new sentences to the draft HR submission for the Opening of School Report her team prepared, she headed to another meeting.

Reflection is a Key to Creating Your Own Personal Roadmap for Transformation

Set aside 45-60 minutes to journal. Reflect, write, review, repeat.

- What feelings emerged for you as read this chapter?
- What ideas sparked for your department or system?
- In your view, in what ways does leadership help or hinder the solutions coming to mind?

Download additional questions at www.EdImperative.org

Cultivating Connections

Mary sat at the dining room table in their new home in Atlanta, sipping a cup of coffee and reading the agenda of activities for the school picnic. She was excited to see a list of icebreakers and activities that would help the students get to know one another before they started the summer skills center and the school year. The activities planned for parents would be a great way to meet some of the people from the school and district, especially the ones who had already been supporting her family. Glancing over at her phone when it began to vibrate, she saw the calendar reminder.

"Sidney! Kya! It's time to go!" Mary called.

"Okay!" the two replied from different parts of the house.

On the drive over to the picnic, Kya played nervously with her squishy stress ball. "What if nobody likes me?"

"You're going to make lots of new friends today, honey," Sidney assured her with his words and a genuine smile reflected in the rearview mirror.

"You're just saying that," Kya replied. "You don't know." Her exuberant personality and self-confidence waned after a tough school year and an emotional move away from her biological father.

As they were turning into the parking lot, Mary reassured her, "Kya, they created this picnic with lots of games and activities so new students like you can get to know other kids and make friends before the school year starts. Just give it a chance. I bet you'll have a lot of fun today."

As they walked toward the school entrance, they were greeted by welcoming faces. "Good morning. We're glad you could make it today. Please check in at the tables ahead. You'll receive name tags and other important information."

As they signed in, a young, energetic girl with bright eyes and braces walked up to Kya. "Hi, my name is Ginny. I'm in the fifth grade. What's your name?"

"Kya," she responded shyly.

"I'm a student volunteer today," Ginny said. "My job is to bring new students into the school for the activities we've got planned this morning. Do you want to come with me?"

Kya looked at her parents with some uncertainty, only to be met with two wide smiles.

"You'll have a great time," Mary assured her.

Ginny chimed in and spoke directly to Sidney and Mary. "The agenda has the pickup time and location, just in case you didn't see it already."

"Thank you," Mary said.

Ginny looked back at Kya. "Are you ready?"

"Yes," she said, gaining confidence, and the two turned and walked away.

"That was nice." Sidney sighed, happy to see his daughter taking chances.

"It was!" Mary agreed.

As they turned back to the registration table, they were greeted by one of the parent volunteers who helped them find their way to their first activity.

Mary and Sidney enjoyed their morning of meeting leaders from the skills center and the school. They were impressed by how the leaders described their work to create one culture between the school and center, in which students participating in the skills center are integrated into the leadership and social fabric of the school. Their faces lit up as the school leadership described their plan for ensuring that all students were mastering the critical content and skills, even if they were doing so at different paces.

After that conversation ended, Mary and Sidney followed the group outside to the lawn, where they participated in an icebreaker with parents and community partners before beginning a series of short activities with each of the community partners. The activities were fun, silly, informative, enriching, and challenging, and they were all examples of experiences that the students would have access to if they participated in the summer or school programs. After the activity ended, Mary and Sidney took a short break and then sat in on a small group conversation with the school and skill center counselors. They were delighted when the counselors talked about attention deficit hyperactivity disorder and attention deficit disorder and described the strategies they use to help students build strong study and organizational skills to support their success.

Time passed quickly as Mary and Sidney engaged in the activities, met many of the individuals who would be supporting Kya, and talked with other parents. They were stunned when one parent described how she had been among the first parents to launch a campaign to create more awareness and urgency around the need to transition to a student-centered district years earlier. "We'd been meeting for almost a year, asking questions of leaders, school staff, and parents, sharing stories, and getting to know more and more parents. With our questions, emails, and responses to district inquiries, we helped to elevate the district's discussion about student-centered transformation that led to the call to action. It's incredible to see where things are today."

Mary and Sidney looked at each other in disbelief. "Ordinary parents with no official role or volunteer assignment were catalysts for this transformation," Mary whispered.

"Wow," Sidney replied.

When Mary saw Kya approaching, she grinned at her daughter, who was perspiring and beaming as she chewed a bite of the pizza she was holding.

"Did you have fun?" Sidney asked.

Kya nodded, her mouth too full to respond otherwise.

"It's time to go." Mary glanced up from her watch.

"Can I go to the park with Vy? She's going tomorrow," Kya said through a smaller mouthful of pizza as a little girl approached them with her mother trailing. "Vy!" She beamed at the sight of her new friend.

Mary and Sidney introduced themselves to Vy and her mother. They talked for a while and made plans for the girls to meet the following day at a nearby park before walking back to their car.

As they drove home, Sidney reflected on the day. "That was fun! The school did a great job of creating activities and icebreakers that made it easy to connect with the other parents. Time really seemed to fly! I really like how thoughtful their approach is to making sure that students have a seamless learning experience between the skill center and school and build community among their peers."

"I felt the same way," Mary replied. "I appreciated hearing the different perspectives on the history of the school, how it was a couple of years ago, and the various steps they took to transform the school into the one we visited today. It's inspiring!"

Sidney hadn't heard all of the history and asked Mary for more details, which she summarized quickly.

"They have come a long way. I'm impressed with their efforts to build community among the families before the school year, and it was also nice to informally meet the summer staff that'll be working with Kya. I wasn't expecting that. And to think this all started with an ordinary group of parents who were relentless in asking questions, sharing stories, and getting other parents involved. Stunning!"

"Kya, what did *you* do?" Mary asked.

"I toured the school and played games, and ate snacks." She was talking fast with excitement.

"Did you meet many kids besides Ginny and Vy?" Sidney asked.

"I met *all* the kids in my different groups. One group will be in my school advisory, and the other group will be in the skill center this summer. We played games to get to know each other. But there were so many kids, I don't remember all their names."

"Well, it sounds like you had a better experience than you thought you would," Mary affirmed.

"I did!" Kya agreed. Her eyes sparkled, and her face lit up with a big grin.

Is this really possible?

How would you get all these individuals to participate in the gathering during the summer? Is this realistic?

Fundamentally, this is a district that has made a commitment to ensuring a strong start to the school year by building community among and relationships between its students, parents, and staff before the school year begins. In fact, it has positioned these interactions as important aspects of the work they are charged with leading and supporting. Many systems believe in and adopt a similar approach. The big questions are: How defined is their community and relationship-building strategy? When does it begin (before the school year or after the start)? What does it entail? How frequently is it reviewed to determine whether continuous improvement opportunities exist to help them better meet target outcomes?

Without question, determining how to implement a similar approach would require significant planning and commitment. A driving question when considering whether to pursue an approach like this one is: What benefits might a stronger school community create for students, families, and teachers? Such an analysis would also require leaders and planning teams to rethink how and when they provide opportunities for staff to recharge.

Determining whether it is possible to implement a similar approach would undoubtedly include a prioritization and cost analysis. This story does not intend to suggest that there will always be enough resources to do everything staff and parents would like, or even everything that individuals believe is needed. However, I am saying that districts need to create planning practices where they have enough advance time to examine their use of resources more holistically so that even in the event of a budget reduction, they have effectively considered whether there are ways to achieve the similar outcomes through reprioritization and a combination of different approaches, including a greater use of partnerships.

Will these offerings really make a difference in improving student outcomes? Given the cost, are there better ways to use the limited resources?

If designed and executed properly, yes! Creating an environment that is focused on healing and building connections is a powerful way to open up lines of dialogue, reshape personal and organizational deficit-driven narratives, and foster understandings that help craft more effective strategies. That said, even with the compelling research that supports this way of thinking, these two questions can best be answered after an organization is both prudent and creative in the designs of a causally connected strategy, does the financial analysis to determine cost, and includes an independent set of eyes, preferably by an organization that has implemented the approach or supported the implementation before.

Why Cultivating Community and Culture Matters to Me

When we were selecting elementary schools for our daughter, there was one private school that impressed us with their expressed commitment to building community among the students and families. They had a number of gatherings, some of which took place before the school year so students could meet and get to know future classmates and parents could form supportive relationships that would make informal gatherings among classmates easier.

As parents, we were assigned a mentor family. They had kids who had been in the school longer, so they could answer basic questions about the school, which made us feel like we had an initial connection to begin our relationship with the school. These opportunities to connect were invaluable and resulted in several long-lasting friendships. When our daughter had a need for additional supports, we already had a good network for identifying the necessary resources to support her, but the majority of these were outside of the school and cost additional money.

Unfortunately, after elementary school, her middle and high schools have not placed an emphasis on building community among parents. My wife and I understand, at least from the school representatives we talked with, that their primary initiative is an effort to help students become more independent and develop the social skills they need to navigate new environments and groups of people. As a parent, I agree with this objective for students but believe the need for a healthy parent community to support students and one another through the schooling years is no less important at the middle and high school level.

In my observation, COVID-19 exacerbated the social connection challenges brought about by this lack of structure and contributed to many students' excessive feelings of isolation. In conversations with other parents, I was struck by how many of their children reported that they were never asked to turn their screen on to introduce themselves or get involved in any activity to help them get to know their classmates or build community while online and even when they were back on campus. Community-building within schools and among students should be an essential component, particularly as the places in which students can participate in learning expand.

After her daughter's first week at the skills center, Mary received a progress report outlining what Kya had been working on in reading and math. She was pleased to see the detailed breakdown of Kya's performance and progress in each area and grateful for the positive feedback on her daughter's participation. She also greatly appreciated the links to tips on how parents can have the most effective dialogue with their children about their performance and do additional practice exercises if they were needed.

When Kya burst into the dining room where Mary was sitting reading the report, she decided to do her own check-in on Kya. "Hi, sweetheart. How was your day at the skills center?"

"It was fun! It's like a summer camp! We played a lot of games. We went outside. We had a fun field trip." Kya's expression and voice were full of enthusiasm.

I love seeing her so happy again! Mary beamed while watching Kya.

"What about your work in math? How is that?" Mary inquired.

"We do some math," Kya responded. "It's okay."

"Do you feel like you understand it better?" Mary asked.

"Yes!" Kya affirmed. "My teachers explain things really well."

Each week, Mary and Sidney received progress reports. These highlighted what Kya was doing well, where she needed improvement, and how it related to the concepts she needed to master to be successful in the fourth grade. They were pleased with her steady progress and her continued interest in attending the skills center. It warmed their hearts to learn about the friendships Kya was developing with a wide range of classmates, which they believe was only possible because of the efforts the center made.

By the end of the summer, Kya had reached grade level in reading and math and was set to attend her assigned school. She was relieved to hear that the school would host events for her student advisory group at the skill center so they could remain connected despite the fact that several students would be attending other schools.

Pleased that Kya had the opportunity to receive the in-depth assistance from a dedicated group of expert teachers focused on helping students close skill gaps, Sidney and Mary were excited about the year ahead for Kya and Chris.

Reflection is a Key to Creating Your Own Personal Roadmap for Transformation

Set aside 45-60 minutes to journal. Reflect, write, review, repeat.

- What feelings emerged for you as read this chapter?

- What ideas sparked for your department or system?

- In your view, in what ways does leadership help or hinder the solutions coming to mind?

Download additional questions at www.EdImperative.org

Learning in a "One System, One School" Ecosystem

O n his first day of school, Chris was guided to board the yellow school bus heading for the orientation camp, per the principal's instructions. As soon as his dad drove away, he pulled his hoodie up, shoved his hands into his pockets, and reluctantly joined the line.

I really don't want to do this, but I promised Dad I'd give it a try. I mean, outdoor school does sound cool, but the wellness center sounds stupid. I don't have anything to talk about. If they think I'm going to talk about losing my mom, they're wrong.

For a brief moment, he was overwhelmed by the same awkwardness and nervousness he felt when he arrived at the summer gathering. But as he stepped onto the bus, all the awkward feelings and overwhelm melted away when he saw Kevin and Pri and remembered the fun they'd had together when they'd met at the summer gathering. Kevin grinned and Pri's face lit up at the sight of Chris, and they waved him over to sit near them. As he took his seat, he breathed a sigh of relief.

I'm glad they're a part of my student advisory group during the school year.

Chris, Kevin, and Pri talked and joked throughout the bus ride, making the time fly by, and they arrived at the campground in what seemed like very little time.

"Good morning, students." A woman's voice came over the bus speaker. "When the bus comes to a stop, please gather your things and meet your student advisor in the center of the field."

As Chris exited the bus, he saw his advisor, Mr. Lopez, as well as a few other students he recognized from the summer picnic, standing in the center of a huge grassy field.

After the students assembled in their advisory groups, a booming voice came over the loudspeakers. "Good morning, scholars! My name is Principal Montgomery. I'm excited to welcome you to the 2022 school year at the Outdoor School! Our mission is to inspire your creativity and learning by building a bridge between the real world and your interests, talents, and skills. As a new school and one that may be very different from what you've previously experienced, we've created this two-day orientation to share our expectations and lay the foundation for our work together this year. Before you break into your advisory groups, I want to talk a little about why we exist as a school and what values we want to hold each other accountable to as a school community."

Chris leaned forward and focused his attention, trying to give these people the chance his dad had asked him to.

"The outdoor school was created to provide a learning experience for students who learn better in a hands-on environment. You'll learn the same concepts that you would in traditional school, but you'll learn them through outdoor experiences and interactions with individuals and organizations inside and mostly outside of the school."

As he listened, Chris noticed that he didn't have the usual pit in his stomach when it came to going to school.

School is so boring! I'd much rather go with Dad to his job at the bank, but maybe this will be okay.

"Your advisory groups are a way for you to develop a trusted relationship with an adult as well as a structured peer support network in the school to support your learning and development throughout the year. Our goal for the student advisory is to create an experience where you feel safe, supported, challenged, and excited about learning. You may be surprised to know that our approach is based on research on how our brains and bodies respond to positive experiences, such as receiving encouragement, and having supports and clear guidelines to help us overcome adverse experiences, such as feeling unsafe socially or academically at school, dealing with death, divorce, or even a parent's job loss."

That explains why I felt like my brain didn't work after Mom died. Feeling connected for the first time in a long time, Chris settled into the experience and listened with more focus.

"You will hear quite a bit about our school's values during this orientation and throughout the school year, and we want this to be a conversation. We want you to ask questions if you don't understand something about our values. We want you to challenge anything you hear if you disagree or think something needs to change. Now, to be clear, that doesn't mean you can disregard a value you don't agree with before we agree to a change, but it does mean we sincerely want you to speak up if you think something is missing. You can also speak up if you find something working really well. In order for our culture to take root and the outdoor school to become the best it can be, we all need to hold each other accountable to living our values.

"We have five values that guide our school culture, which you'll find spelled out on the notecard we're handing out. They are:

- **Mindfulness.** We learn and use mindfulness techniques to ensure healthy, positive interactions with ourselves and others and to determine how to have bold conversations that bring about the change we hope to see in the world.

- **Responsibility.** We expect our students to take responsibility for their learning and become resourceful, motivated, and independent learners who are skilled at engaging teachers, staff, parents, and peers as resources to advance their education.

- **Empowerment.** Our students, parents, and staff are encouraged and empowered to speak up about issues that are important to them and collaborate on solving problems.

- **Exploration.** Our students and teachers are curious. They use their curiosity to fuel their inquiry, dialogue, analysis, and evaluations associated with their learning plans.

- **Inclusivity and Equity.** Our students, staff, and parents believe in creating learning and social environments and interactions that are diverse, inclusive, equitable, and rewarding for all participants.

Chris was intrigued.

"You may have heard that the district will be offering additional supports to students via the wellness and skills centers. Students will be moving in and out of these centers while staying connected to their home school. It is important to me, our school staff, your parents, and our district leadership that you all understand that our centers and schools are intended to function as ONE school community."

How does that work? Won't people look at us funny? Chris wondered.

As if he'd heard the question in Chris's mind, the man answered his concern. "In other districts, and even in this district in recent years, you may have heard students make jokes about students who participated in certain programs, have certain learning or developmental needs, et cetera. Well, that stops today. While it was *never* a part of our desired school or district culture, it became a part of our informal culture because we did not create the necessary supports to hold ourselves accountable to a higher standard. My goal, and I want you to have this as your goal as well, is to put that practice to an end."

I like the idea of doing that, but I don't know what I can do to help put an end to it. I'm just a kid.

"The teachers who have come together to create the Outdoor School want you to have the *best* learning environment to stimulate your curiosity, cultivate your talents and skills, and grow academically and socially. Along the way, you and we will experience challenges, disappointments, setbacks, and other stressors that add complexity to the learning environment. What do I mean by this? You might not demonstrate a mastery of concepts and skills as quickly as you would like, you may have a very sick family member, you could have a close relative lose a job or have difficulty finding a job, et cetera. In the outdoor school, we are supportive of one another and do not tolerate intimidation of others when it comes to their learning differences, life circumstances, or differences in general. We support each of you, our school staff, and parent community in your respective efforts to better yourselves. Like a center for individuals who want to hone and perfect their craft, the skills center is designed and intended to help students who need or want help mastering the concepts and skills. Similarly, the wellness center is there for individuals who are dealing with life circumstances that may be overwhelming and interfering with their ability to learn. You may have heard the saying, 'it takes a village to raise a child.' Our school, the centers, our teachers and you students are a part of *one* village."

Interesting. I'll be surprised if they can pull this off, but it'll be awesome if they do, Chris thought, creating a little space between his doubt and what he hoped was possible.

"In just a few moments, you will break into your advisory groups to ask questions you may have. You will also participate in activities and discussions that help bring these expectations to life in ways that are relevant and helpful in your daily interactions with your student advisory groups, the skills center, and the wellness center. When you're finished, we'll reconvene as one big group and share some of the things you discuss in your advisories."

After locating Mr. Lopez and his group, Chris found a comfortable spot to sit and listen.

"Good morning! My name is Mr. Lopez. I'm your eighth-grade student advisor and one of the teachers responsible for your math curriculum. I've been a teacher for eight years and applied to be a teacher in the outdoor school because I *love* applied learning environments and believe you can learn a lot about math outside of the school walls that will serve you well as you progress in school and life. We have two objectives for our time together this morning. First, to discuss your expectations for the school culture and student leadership within it. Second, to discuss your thoughts on how we can best maintain a One School culture." He smiled. "Let's get started by introducing ourselves. Please share your first and last name, why you chose to attend the outdoor school, and one fun thing you did over the summer."

Each student hesitantly introduced themselves, and Mr. Lopez quickly caught the themes that these students felt the traditional classroom did not capture their interests, support their desired learning style, or meet their learning needs.

"Thank you for sharing. I'm glad each of you is here, and I know this is going to be your best school year ever." His grin spread from ear to ear. "Now, we're going to spend some time identifying what an ideal school environment looks like and doesn't look like from your perspective. Every advisory is doing this activity, and we're going to use what we learn here to create a school culture charter that we live by as a school."

We get to help make the rules? Chris mused. *Interesting.*

"First, I want to give you a little time to think privately about this. Here are some prompts," Mr. Lopez said as he passed out worksheets to each student. "These should help you think through how you really feel about school and the type of school you want to co-create with us. When you're done thinking on your own, I'll ask you to partner with someone you don't already know to share your thoughts."

Chris looked over the worksheet. His eyes were drawn to two questions: What could we do to make school a fun and exciting place where you can't wait to go every day? What about your experiences at previous schools didn't you like?

Wow, I don't think anyone has ever asked me for my thoughts about school, except my parents. He picked up the pencil Mr. Lopez had given him and started writing.

After the group heard and read some of their feedback, Chris felt a rush of excitement and wonder come over him.

A school like the one we're working to build would be awesome! I wonder if they'll actually follow through on this. I've had lots of teachers and staff make promises they didn't keep.

"What does student leadership look like in the school culture you described?" Mr. Lopez paused for a response. When he was met with silence, he smiled again and handed a sheet of paper to each student. "Take five minutes to read these stories about how other students have demonstrated leadership at their schools. Jot down what stands out to you about their leadership, and then we'll share."

Five minutes later, Mr. Lopez asked, "Okay, time's up. What did you learn?"

Pri was the first to speak up. "One student engaged her school community in a global campaign to support ocean health."

"The student I read about rallied her class and school leadership to address cyberbullying," said Matt.

"The student I read about volunteered to read stories to preschool students during lunchtime," added Kevin.

When each student finished sharing, Mr. Lopez asked, "What stands out to you about these stories?"

"You can demonstrate leadership in so many different ways," offered Kevin.

"I agree," chimed in Chris, as others nodded in agreement.

After a few other students shared, Mr. Lopez continued, "Great! Now, I want you to break into pairs. I'd like each of you to take five minutes to write down a story that best describes how *you* have shown leadership that made a difference for someone else at school, home, or elsewhere. And make sure you share the context, your role, the outcome, and what stood out most to you about that experience."

It took a moment for Chris to come up with his example, but he was happy about the one he chose. He felt a deep sense of pride well up in his chest as he shared the story of standing up for his stepsister at the movie theater when a group of kids were teasing her for her exuberance. He recalled walking over to the kids, a mix of boys and girls about his age, and saying, "We've all had our moments when we've been excited about something. Why are you trying to hurt the feelings of this little kid you don't even know?" He had said it with a calm but very stern look. What stood out most to him was that he wasn't afraid when he thought he otherwise would be. In that moment, he felt strongly that their behavior was wrong, and he wanted to say something about it. To his surprise, the group of kids didn't argue back. One of them even apologized to him and walked over to Kya and apologized to her too. Chris thanked the girl and the group and walked back to Kya, who gave him a big hug.

After the pairs had shared with one another, Mr. Lopez asked each student to share their partner's story with excitement, focusing on what was remarkable about their leadership.

The kids really got into it, obviously inspired by their peers' stories.

"You've done a nice job sharing and working together," said Mr. Lopez. "Now, we are going to take a fifteen-minute break."

Chris, Pri, and Kevin stood up and quickly decided to walk down to the creek together.

"I've *never* experienced anything like this before," said Chris.

"Me either," Kevin agreed.

"It's kind of cool," said Pri. "I'm excited to see where it goes."

They checked out the stream and skipped a couple of rocks before hustling back when they heard the callback over the speakers.

Mr. Lopez got right back into it. "We have just an hour or so before we reconvene with the other students. Before we meet back up with them, I want to spend some time talking about the skills center and wellness center, answering your questions and setting our expectations. As you meet more of your peers, you'll notice that there are many students moving in and out of both centers. I want you to take sixty seconds to jot down your questions about the centers and put them in the hat that will be passed around. I'll read and answer each question."

When the hat was full, Mr. Lopez pulled each question out and read it aloud.

"How will students stay connected to the school and advisory when they're at a center?"

"How will students keep up with what's going on at the school?"

"If a student is in the skills center, does that mean they're stupid?"

"What if I don't want people to know I'm in the skills center because I'm embarrassed?"

"What if I don't want people to know I'm going to the wellness center?"

"These are all really good questions," Mr. Lopez said and began passing the hat again. "The hat is being passed again, just in case you have any additional questions." He looked pleased. The school and Learning Options Task Force elicited questions and responses that enabled him to confidently answer the student's questions.

After answering each of the questions, he invited them to give more feedback. "You've heard the responses we have discussed as a school staff. Now, I'd like to hear *your* responses to a few of the questions you asked. You may have ideas we can add. So, how would you answer these questions: If you are attending one of the centers, how would you like to stay informed of what's going on at the school? And how would you like students to respect your privacy if they learn you were participating in one of the centers?"

The students answered the questions enthusiastically.

"Those were all great ideas, and I'll be bringing them back to the staff to discuss and integrate. We're going to have a great year together. Now, let's get back to the big group!"

Chris was less enthusiastic as he slowly made his way to the picnic table underneath a shelter to meet his second advisor and student advisory group for lunch. This group of six other students from his school would also be attending the wellness center. He recognized one of the students from the summer gathering, and even though they didn't know each other well, it was nice to see a familiar face.

"Hello, Chris," said Ms. Steffan, the counselor and advisor from the wellness center. "It's nice to meet you."

"Hi," Chris responded, noticing how relaxed he felt in the presence of this cheerful woman who was dressed very differently than all the other teachers in a bright orange flowy dress. He could feel her genuine care somehow, even in just her greeting.

As the students ate their lunches, she introduced herself. "My name is Ms. Steffan. I'm a counselor at the wellness center and have been a counselor within Phoenix County School District for ten years. After supporting students academically at the elementary, middle, and high school levels, I came to the wellness center because I've seen a lot of students over the years who have had painful, traumatic experiences occur in their life and not much support to deal with them. I was thrilled to hear about the superintendent's recommendation and school board's decision to create a wellness center to give students support during very difficult life circumstances."

It's been much harder for me to concentrate in school since my mom died, Chris admitted to himself. He looked around the table and wondered what the other students had been through.

"The purpose of the wellness center is to partner with families and teachers to make sure your wellness and learning are considered together during specific moments. The center has three goals.

"First, we provide you and your family with structure and information that can help you develop, strengthen, and use a practice of ongoing self-care to foster your well-being during every stage of your life.

"Second, we ensure your school supports your family's priorities for your wellness and develops a tailored educational plan that supports you in learning the materials at a flexible pace while you are dealing with difficult life circumstances.

"Third, we give you the space and supports you need to begin to heal so you can return to the activities you were engaged in before the crisis happened."

As Ms. Steffan spoke, she scanned the group, making eye contact with each student and checking body language to ensure understanding. Seeing some uncertainty, she continued. "We all recognize school as the place where kids go to learn to read and write. We also recognize that individuals go to a doctor to deal with health problems, and they go to a mechanic to deal with car problems. When people experience events that cause emotional turmoil, some go to a counselor temporarily, but many do not get support to deal with the impact of those events on their thoughts, feelings, and body. We know a lot about how the brain and body deal with painful events and what it takes to reduce the pain in healthy ways. The wellness center teaches those skills. You all will benefit from those lessons like I have, because, at one time or another, everyone in the world deals with disappointing, painful, traumatic life events."

Everyone will deal with a situation like this? Yeah, I guess that's true. We'll all learn how to manage the hard stuff and I won't be singled out. Chris's shoulders relaxed, and his discomfort about the wellness center, being singled out as different and being forced into "touchy-feely stuff" began to disappear. He breathed a big sigh of relief. *I wonder what kinds of strategies they'll teach me that'll help me deal with the pain of losing my mom. It still feels terrible, and it hasn't gotten any better.*

"When you are enrolled in the wellness center, I will be the liaison between you, your parents, and your school advisor. Your teachers at the wellness center and outdoor school will work together to develop an education plan that helps you learn the materials being taught at a pace that meets your needs, and we'll be providing your parents with weekly progress reports during your rotation through the wellness center. Do any of you have questions?"

"When will we see our school student advisory?" asked Chris.

"Great question! Student advisories meet weekly. You will participate in half of the advisories virtually and half in person," she responded. "You will also receive the daily school announcements, invitations for all school events, and sign-ups for extracurricular activities. Student government elections will be held soon, so you'll have an opportunity to run for office too."

Chris could see some of the other students smile and show similar signs of relief as they learned that they would have access to all the information, events, and opportunities taking place at school.

Okay, now I'm excited about all of this! If they actually do what they say. Maybe this can be my best school year ever.

Is this really possible?

Won't the skills center create the same social stigma that existed with traditional tracking and the pull-out intervention model that has had mixed results at best?

No. As stated previously, I believe this is far less likely to occur because at each phase of interaction with key processes and staff, this district is demonstrating a One System, One School formal and informal culture—a culture that recognizes and embraces that, at some point, students may have different needs and need to take additional steps to address them. Through its master schedule planning, staffing assignments, and organization, this system has a well-conceived plan for keeping students connected to their various school communities. These objectives are facilitated by their early and frequent efforts to build authentic, genuine community among students and families as well as their ability to show clear, noteworthy improvement. Because of its consistency, accountability, and empowerment, I believe students will buy into the culture and honor its values. A skills center should be designed with a focus on how to best support students with identified needs, and its effectiveness should be judged by its consistency in helping students improve and re-enter their class at grade level at an acceptable cost.

Are you doing students a disservice by making special accommodations for them in the wellness center when those accommodations will not always be available in life? Moreover, people don't heal on a schedule, so how will the wellness center measure its effectiveness?

First and foremost, this aspirational district values the well-being of its students, staff, and community and, through its example, prioritizes helping students develop an appreciation and practice of self-care and self-improvement. Such a foundation is important for all students as they navigate a complex, stressful world in which self-care and self-improvement will continue to be essential to their health and survival.

This aspirational wellness center in no way suggests or promises that students will be "healed" before their rotation ends. It does promise, however, that students would learn some foundational coping strategies and receive daily structure and supports that aid the healing process if they are deemed by their parents and care professionals to need such a space. This approach would benefit the brain development and life trajectory of many students who do not have such a support infrastructure. According to the Substance Abuse and Mental Health Services Administration (SAMSHA), more than two-thirds of children reported at least one traumatic event by age sixteen.[26] Additionally, SAMSHA reports that the impact of traumatic stress can last well beyond childhood, leading to learning problems (lower grades, suspensions, expulsions), increased use of health and mental health services, increased involvement in child welfare and juvenile justice systems, and even long-term health problems (diabetes and heart disease). The wellness center is a vision for providing significantly more students with tools, practices, and a space to learn how to heal so they can move forward in their lives in a healthy, productive manner.

The learning time and environment seem so different from today. Doesn't this amount to a lot of lost instructional time?

These aspirational practices would not amount to lost instructional time but rather result in *more* instructional time. When systems are designed to support students' emotional well-being and students also have the tools and skills they need to self-regulate, there will be fewer behavioral issues and more productive learning time as students can rely on the collective energy of their peers in a healthier learning environment.

Why Whole Student Success Matters to Me

In my experience as a district leader, parent, student teacher, and student, I have observed that it is essential for students to keep pace with the daily instruction. Otherwise, the amount of material a student has to make up will continue to grow, and the supports provided by the school will dwindle. I have heard many stories of students falling so far behind that they stop trying, never catch up, develop a negative self-narrative, and even stop going to school. This reality, in my view, is in part due to a design assumption that students' needs will be met by the academic and interventions in place to support them.

When I was deputy superintendent, I often wondered how many students were falling too far behind because they were functioning below their normal levels or caught in a downward spiral due to a traumatic event related to the death of a loved one, a divorce, personal illness, or difficulty managing their learning differences. I was curious about how well families thought we were supporting their child during those difficult life events. I also reflected on how many well-intentioned yet punitive motivational incentives contributed to students feeling overwhelmed.

And students were not the only ones dealing with challenging life circumstances. I thought a lot about how our learning and work environments were impacted by staff powering through as caregivers, or dealing with health issues, or facing other extenuating factors. I often wondered what would happen if there were an initiative aimed at shifting our culture to one where wellness was supported and emphasized. I am certain that many colleagues received verbal messages encouraging them to take care of themselves and to take time off if needed, but it seemed like those offers occurred once someone was depleted rather than as a supportive preventive measure.

I left the district thinking that if I ever joined another one, having a well-designed wellness program would be one of the first initiatives I would put in place to ensure the self-care and well-being of students and staff. Since we have entered the season of COVID-19, I believe such an initiative is more important than ever.

After dinner, Mary and Sidney finally had a moment to talk about the curriculum night they had just attended at the outdoor school. They had both been eager to participate. School had been in session for a month, and they were intrigued by Chris's positive, albeit limited, comments about his experience.

"Well," Sidney started as they began their nighttime routine. "I have to tell you, it thrilled me to hear Chris rave about orientation camp and his experience at the wellness center. And I've been impressed and pleased with the weekly reports we've been receiving. At the beginning, I thought this was the best option for Chris, but I still questioned whether the combination of the outdoor school and wellness center would provide the rigorous learning experience I wanted for him." His face brightened as he unbuttoned his collar. "But after what I've heard so far, I don't have that concern anymore. This district continues to amaze me."

"I know!" Mary agreed. "They have definitely created something special there. I love the way they introduce us to the other families. I really think we should reach out to the Larsons. They are so lovely, and their son and Chris would really hit it off." Mary moisturized her hands and arms as she spoke. "And I loved the crosswalk they built to show us what a lesson might look like in a traditional class versus the outdoor school. It's much more hands-on. It requires navigating a variety of academic, professional, and civic environments. And it has much more interaction with people outside of school. And did you see the models of what they expect of the students' work?" Her eyes were wide with awe. "I can see why Chris is thriving there."

"Yes." He nodded. "That blew me away. The rigor of the assignments and the layers of support available to ensure every student is mastering the material rather than just simply finishing an assignment. I mean, shoot, that kind of structure should be in every school, not just the outdoor school."

"Right, I agree. And the student intervention teams have an excellent plan for helping students achieve mastery and practice self-care, which is so wonderful. It looks to me like they work seamlessly with the advisories. It's all so… " she searched for the right word as she pulled back the sheets, "thoughtful, with the curricula in all the centers and the coordination between everyone responsible for the kids' learning and well-being."

"I wish I would have had those types of supports when I was in school. This community holding our children's future in their hands seems so caring and trustworthy. Having something like this would have made all the difference for me when I was dealing with my childhood issues." He paused, clearly overcome with emotion, which was unusual for him. "Mary, I am so grateful we found this system for our children."

"Me too, honey. Me too. I look forward to meeting with Ms. Steffan and Chris at our check-in and to hearing what the rest of his year will look like."

Mary grabbed a notepad off her nightstand to jot down a few thoughts she had about Chris's experience at the outdoor school orientation camp and their experience at curriculum night. She knew the Learning Options Task Force would reconvene in a few days to review a draft parent survey intended to elicit responses about the curriculum instruction and student learning; perceptions of supports provided to students, teachers, and families; and questions that would help them understand if families felt their student was more engaged and motivated as a result of the new learning opportunity. Knowing the survey results would be discussed among the district's curriculum team, school oversight teams, and in the board's curriculum and instruction committee, she wanted to make sure she was prepared to share her experience, ask questions, and offer her best thinking.

The planned six-week rotation through the wellness center was coming to an end, and it was time for Sidney, Mary, and Chris to meet with Ms. Steffan.

"I'm so glad to see you," Ms. Steffan began. "Sidney and Mary, it has been an absolute pleasure to have Chris join us at the wellness center. As you know, the purpose of this meeting is to discuss if the rotation should continue or if he's ready to transition back to school. Chris, I'd love for you to start us off by sharing your experience here."

As Chris talked about the activities and the work he had done through the socio-emotional curriculum, Mary and Sidney sat in awe—truly amazed that he could speak so clearly about how he had been feeling since his mother's passing and the strategies he had learned to help deal with those feelings. He talked about the breathing techniques, the nature walks, the meditations, and the different religious and philosophical perspectives on death he had discovered and found useful. He also shared what he had learned about the impact of trauma on the brain and the body.

"I still have moments when I feel really sad, but I think I'm ready to get back to school. I feel better than I have in a long time. Plus, I'm only a couple of lessons behind where the rest of my class is, and I believe I can catch up."

"When Chris leaves the wellness center, will all of his supports end?" Mary asked Ms. Steffan.

"Good question," the counselor replied. "No, Chris and I will check in monthly for the remainder of the school year, and Chris will remain a part of his wellness center student advisory. They will continue to have weekly check-ins, work through the curriculum, and have a peer group that supports one another for at least another six weeks to ease the transition back into the classroom. We have a check-in at the end of that period to determine appropriate next steps."

Mary and Sidney glanced at each other, their faces relaxed.

"That's good to hear," Sidney shared.

Chris nodded. "Yeah, I probably wouldn't feel ready if I didn't have those in place."

With no more questions for Chris, he left the room, giving Mary and Sidney an opportunity to talk privately with Ms. Steffan. They were eager to learn more about where she had seen Chris have breakthroughs and where she felt support was still needed.

"Around the house, his mood is better and he's more available, but he still doesn't talk much about how he's doing," Mary shared.

Ms. Steffan continued. "You know, Chris really took to reading about the different religious and historical perspectives on death, and how the brain and body deal with trauma. He actively participated in the strategies, and he truly seemed to value the nature walks. He processes a lot on his own, but we've seen growth in his readiness to engage. We expect he'll feel even more comfortable as he continues to focus on his healing in an environment designed to support his well-being."

"That's reassuring. I'm just so grateful for all you have already done to support him," Sidney commented.

"Well, like I said, it's been our pleasure. Chris is a wonderful boy, and his entire support team agrees that he's ready to return to school. As next steps, we'll let his home school know that he's ready to return full-time next week. The student intervention team will meet to develop a reentry plan to support him with getting caught up with the class, and you and he will receive a copy of the plan before the transition is finalized. Once we sign off on it, the transition will take place."

"That sounds perfect," Mary said, and Sidney nodded in approval.

"Thank you so much for all you've done. We're just so happy that this resource is available for him and other students," Sidney said.

"I am too," said Ms. Steffan with a smile.

Reflection is a Key to Creating Your Own Personal Roadmap for Transformation

Set aside 45-60 minutes to journal. Reflect, write, review, repeat.

- What feelings emerged for you as read this chapter?

- What ideas sparked for your department or system?

- In your view, in what ways does leadership help or hinder the solutions coming to mind?

Download additional questions at www.EdImperative.org

Collaborating with Constructive Feedback

Reaching the final slide of her presentation, third-grade teacher Joelle Ku flipped to the Q&A slide.

"Do you have any additional questions I can answer?" she asked the room full of parents.

A woman's hand shot into the air.

"Yes!" Joelle made eye contact with her and invited her to speak.

"Thank you for your presentation. It was very informative and well-organized." The woman paused and squirmed a bit. "I don't mean for my question to sound offensive, so please bear with me. I know our district has been working on this new approach for a few years, and you mentioned this is your first year here. I guess I'm wondering how prepared you are to be successful in our system given all the ways we have recently changed?" the woman questioned, thinking both as a parent with children who had been in the district for ten years and as a member of a family that had attended district schools for decades.

"In my fifteen years as a teacher working in three different districts, I've never seen anything like this one! Even the new teacher orientation I attended just a couple of weeks ago was the best, most comprehensive, and welcoming experience I've ever had in a school system." Her eyes sparkled as she recalled the memories.

"All four hundred new teachers met for a kickoff orientation meeting and welcome event. The day was very well-organized. I was intentionally seated next to new teachers from the other outdoor schools, neighboring schools, wellness centers, and skill centers in my geographic region. In my personalized folder, I found the bios of my tablemates, a summary of the district leaders' roles and responsibilities, a list of key contacts, FAQs, a history of the district and an overview of its culture, a summary of the core student support processes and systems, an overview of the various feedback loops that have been created to ensure teachers' voices are captured and used to inform planning, delivery, and evaluation of success at the central office level, and a schedule of technology trainings and other new teacher-related trainings and meetings for the entire school year. We spent the day going over that information and meeting the leaders who are responsible for supporting us. It was very informative and inspiring."

Joelle connected with all the parents in the room as she shared her incredible experience of the care and systems within this district. "During the second half of the day, we met in school teams and in peer school teams to learn about the professional learning communities we will be a part of during the year. Then we received our student rosters with a summary of information and interests taken from the enrollment forms you completed for your children. Every one of your children has been placed with a teacher whose personality and capacities are a very good match for them." She paused, smiling broadly. "I have never been in a district that used this approach with central office and community supports aligned to help *me* meet the needs of my students, especially those whose needs require more than I can offer via my role in the classroom.

I'm very excited about it! Usually we receive our students randomly. We do our best to meet their needs, but in all honesty, sometimes it's not a good match. We're often left alone in the classroom to support our students as best we can. Central office and community support are often not aligned, if support is provided at all. All of this makes for a very difficult experience for the student and the teacher."

She shook her head in wonder as she reflected on it all. "When I began the day, I was nervous about what to expect as a new teacher to the district and, if I'm honest, a little doubtful that the district could actually pull this off." She briefly recalled reading the discussion of the district practices put in place to become a learning organization.

Practices that Support Our Efforts to Grow as a Learning Organization

- **Instructional Rounds**. Provides educators across the district a structure and practice for discussing what high-quality instruction looks like and working collaboratively to create a culture of continuous improvement.

- **Service Improvement Cycle**. Teachers participate in the central office satisfaction survey, which captures stakeholder feedback on the customer service, service delivery processes, communications, and trainings of each department that supports teachers and students. The focus groups that are held afterward provide qualitative stakeholder insights about the areas deemed most critical to address in the departments receiving the lowest survey ratings. Insights shared in the focus groups inform midyear course corrections and action-planning and budget requests for the next school year.

- **Data Reviews.** Educators participate in structured data analysis discussions with one another, and occasionally a member of the district's research and assessment team, to unpack performance trends, explore training needs, and support strategies for students, teachers, and instructional program teams. These reviews discuss the results of rapid Plan-Do-Study-Act (PDSA) learning cycles and empathy interviews to inform practices and process improvements.

- **Master Teacher Online Chat.** The online chat system records and analyzes chats, providing daily and weekly reports on the most frequent terms used. Master teachers use this data to analyze trends that inform the district's training, professional development, and instructional rounds agenda.

- **Budget Planning Process.** Educators participate in their school budgeting process and, through their feedback on programs, all their concerns, insights, and suggestions are used to inform central office budget planning.

- **Wellness Scorecard.** Educators and system leaders regularly examine schools and the district's wellness scorecard to determine whether staff and student well-being, school climate, and the work environment are being maintained in a manner that reflects the desired mindful, trauma-informed culture. There are regular opportunities for stakeholders to participate in a light-touch manner. Reviews are held quarterly. Action is taken immediately.

- **Work Groups and Advisory Committees.** Educators at all experience levels are invited to participate in a range of work groups and advisory committees at the school, region, central office, community, state, and national levels to monitor, examine, and make recommendations for improvements to practices and processes that guide management.

"By the end of the day, and after our informal mixer at Lincoln Park, I clearly understood what they expected of me and how we would work together to support students. Plus, I had met several people who I deeply connected with and look forward to getting to know better." Her confidence and enthusiasm were contagious.

"Someone here has listened to teachers and developed an orientation that seems to have thought about every support a teacher would need to be successful in helping *your* children achieve their potential," Joelle said. "Personally, I'm thrilled to see how much more I can offer your children and you, all because of the support and resources I have at my fingertips."

"That's incredible," Mary said with a smile, glancing at Sidney, whose body language also showed approval. "Thank you for sharing that context."

"You're welcome. And, let me be clear, while I'm amazed and believe I'll continue to be, I still expect there will be some challenges. I am confident, however, that the people in this district are tuned in and ready to listen and make necessary adjustments to the systems and processes as needs arise."

Joelle answered a couple of additional questions before wrapping up the meeting.

"Thank you for taking the time to attend curriculum night. If you have additional questions, please feel free to email me or find me after you've visited the other stations this evening. I'll be here for a few minutes after all the presentations are completed."

As they walked toward the exit, Mary grabbed Sidney's hand and said, "It was great to hear a firsthand account of a teacher's experience with the new learning options since a good portion of our work on the task force is dealing with administrators. There are so many moving parts in the district. I'm so impressed with how well-organized they are and how each area is designed with the main stakeholders in mind."

Three days later, Joelle grabbed her laptop and joined the staff in the auditorium for a forty-five-minute after-action review to discuss what went well and what could have been improved during curriculum night.

Ms. Wilson, the school principal, greeted the staff and turned the meeting over to Ms. Lewis, a second-grade teacher, department head, and facilitator of the after-action review. Joelle liked that the role rotated so that there would be multiple opportunities for interested individuals to serve as a facilitator.

"Good afternoon," Ms. Lewis greeted the group with her usual upbeat energy. "Before we begin our dialogue, please take five minutes to reflect briefly on the questions posted on the screen."

Joelle read the list:

- What were the highlights from the curriculum night?
- Were you asked any questions you were not comfortable answering?
- Did parents ask any questions or express any concerns that you believe require immediate follow-up?

- Were you able to build connections with each family? What worked well and didn't work well in your attempts to achieve that goal? Do you recall any moments where you felt triggered or had to assess your own assumptions as you interacted with families?

- Did you see any opportunities to improve curriculum night going forward?

"Let's come back together." Ms. Lewis gently brought everyone back to attention. "Now, let's take ten minutes to write brief responses to the questions. Please navigate to our collaborative workspace using the link you've been provided, and include only one idea per sticky note."

Per her instructions, the team began populating a collaborative document in which they could each write brief responses to the questions on the list. After ten minutes, Ms. Lewis facilitated a brief discussion around the themes the team identified in response to each question.

About ten minutes before the meeting ended, Ms. Lewis asked the notetaker to post the list of key takeaways from the night that the group had developed.

Ms. Wilson remarked, "You did an excellent job putting together a night that engaged families, built community, and provided a deeper understanding of how we're preparing their children for academic and social success. I was very pleased to see that so many of our families who speak English as a second language attended, and I share your belief that our staff and translators did a great job of creating icebreakers that built community among all of our families. I also appreciate your candid feedback that I need to temper my enthusiasm and ensure more time is left for parents to ask the leadership team questions." Her smile was genuine.

Joelle was amazed. She had never worked in an environment that appeared so open, where it was safe to provide constructive feedback to a supervisor...in a staff meeting. She turned to her neighbor and whispered with excitement, "I've never used the after-action review protocol before, but I can see its value in helping the team continuously improve."

"We will be keeping the lessons we've learned from our after-action reviews in our shared folder," Ms. Lewis commented. "They'll be organized by event subfolders and available for anyone to access at any time. Okay, thank you for your time, and have a wonderful rest of the day. We are adjourned."

Joelle was very pleased to hear that these notes would be accessible; she planned to use them to prepare for her next curriculum night.

A few weeks later, when she was reviewing her schedule for the week, Joelle saw there was a Professional Learning Community (PLC) meeting on the calendar. She quickly pulled out her PLC binder and reviewed the summary provided at the new teacher orientation.

Professional Learning Community Resources for Teachers

- **Mentor Teachers.** Each teacher new to the profession has a master teacher in their school who will support them as a mentor teacher. Their role is to help the new teacher acclimate to the school and answer basic instructional questions that support their transition and integration into the school community.

- **Instructional Rounds.** This practice, taken from the medical field, allows educators to develop a shared understanding of what high-quality instruction looks like by providing opportunities for them to observe teachers by school, grade, and region and then discuss and compare their own instructional practices. Instructional rounds are not evaluative or intended to give feedback to the teacher being observed, unless they request it.

- **Training.** Trainings will be held on each curriculum and technology solution to provide all teachers with a foundational understanding and opportunities to observe, share, and discuss effective practices for the various types of students the district educates.

- **Professional Development.** These events include conversations with experts and authors intended to enhance and enrich the school and district culture.

- **Learning Platform.** Teachers have access to a learning platform that curates effective practices from classrooms and school districts around the country.

- **Formal Evaluation.** Common themes from teacher evaluations relevant to the teaching core are aggregated and shared. Teachers work together to understand the factors driving particular outcomes and develop plans for continuously improving their shared practice.

As she scanned the summary, her heart expanded with gratitude when she saw that the district had developed an estimated range of hours teachers would need to spend to reach proficiency in each area and laid out a schedule so the professional learning opportunities would not be too overwhelming. Vividly recalling the challenges she'd had in her previous district trying to find the time for professional development, she was very pleased that the teachers' union and central office team had reached this agreement.

They've thought of everything, Joelle mused.

She was grateful that not every feedback loop was mandatory and appreciated that some opportunities were part of their teacher duties, others were voluntary, and others came with additional stipends.

As she reviewed the schedule, she was excited to see that it would be an instructional rounds meeting.

Great! Off to my first student session.

Later that day, Joelle logged in to the progress monitoring meeting to discuss Kya's progress with her student advisor prior to the parent-teacher conference. She was anticipating a positive conversation because Kya had had a very productive summer in the skills center, increasing her performance to grade level in reading and math by the end of the six-week rotation.

"Hello, Victor. It's nice to see you," Joelle greeted Kya's advisor.

"Hello, Joelle. How are you?" His curiosity matched his attentive expression and posture.

After catching up briefly, they turned their attention to Kya and her performance profile on the screen.

"Wow! Kya appears to have hit her stride and is thriving in school," said Victor, his usually soft-spoken voice more enthusiastic than Joelle had ever heard it. "Her academic performance, wellness scores, school climate responses, teachers' comments, and attendance are all very, very positive."

"Yes, Kya continues to improve her executive functioning skills," Joelle affirmed. "She still participates in weekly meetings to improve her organizational and study skills, and her parents have shared that they are pleased with the additional support and its impact on Kya's work."

"Great!" exclaimed Victor. "I'm sure her parents will be pleased to hear this news. Let's discuss what she needs to focus on next…"

A few minutes later, Joelle thanked Victor for his time and suggestions and logged off from the meeting.

Is this really possible?

Will leaders really support a culture in which their direct reports and peers can provide candid, constructive feedback?

While it may be significantly different from the culture some leaders are accustomed to and the life experiences many leaders have had, many organizations and leaders strive to create a work environment where leaders and staff can provide feedback, admit mistakes, and ask questions without fear of punishment or humiliation. This type of work environment is referred to as a "psychologically safe" environment in the literature. For school systems that do not already have this work environment, I believe most would embrace it if it were set as an expectation and modeled by the most senior leaders and board members. When leaders see the impact such a culture has on empowering others, catalyzing transformation, and enhancing their own leadership, they will be even more inspired.

Changing culture will not happen overnight, but with vision, intention, and perseverance, a new culture will take root. It will require an intentional organizational change management plan with clear expectations, supports, and time for individuals to rewire brain patterns, change habits, and build the trust necessary to enable lasting culture change. Additionally, teams may benefit from some professional development to help individuals recognize their biases, triggers, and blind spots and better understand how past experiences may influence how they escalate or de-escalate specific situations. Teams may also benefit from training in strategies for having crucial conversations with others, especially when emotions are high and perspectives are divergent. With these tools, individuals have a higher likelihood of keeping conversations constructive and building momentum to shift the culture.

Will individuals really be honest about where they feel triggered and the biases they may feel? That seems risky. Is it realistic to think a school district can build that level of trust in its culture?

Yes, based on my experience in a variety of school systems, building trust will require a good deal of work, leadership, vulnerability, relationship-building, listening, and consistent action, among other things. However, it is possible and will pay off in the end with a stronger, healthier environment for adults to work and students to learn.

Trust is often broken and eroded by direct interactions with individuals and the systems put in place to support them. There may be historical patterns of interactions that trigger traumas that families or communities have experienced, and those may require some intentional repairing and healing before trust can be fully restored. Leaders' willingness to consider these needs and make the necessary space to have those conversations will play an important role in determining whether such a culture will be possible districtwide. It doesn't end there though. Trust can also be broken through a wide variety of experiences internal and external stakeholders have with the *processes* intended to support them. When information is shared too late, when a promise is broken due to budget constraints followed by poor communication about it, when there is staff turnover and no one follows up on a commitment, when you are struggling to keep up as a staff or parent and the actions of the organization do not seem to be thinking about your needs, it can feel like trust is being broken.

Organizations must be willing to have a candid stakeholder assessment of their culture to determine what perceptions, behaviors, practices, and systemic weaknesses exist that may serve as impediments to building a culture where trust is high and staff can contribute ideas without fear of punishment or humiliation.

Why Collaboration and Constructive Feedback Matter to Me

As deputy superintendent, one of my primary goals was to help our school leaders and central office leadership team function as a high-performing team. A blog I shared and frequently referred to was the *10 Characteristics of High-Performing Teams*. One of the foundational characteristics included was, *"People have solid and deep trust in each other and in the team's purpose—they feel free to express feelings and ideas."*[27]

I strived to model that attribute by making the *why* behind decisions clear, establishing deadlines around key priorities, keeping and managing expectations around timing of commitments, and publicly owning where I made a mistake or didn't keep a promise and correcting it. While I was far from perfect, in time, I could see that others felt more comfortable doing the same. I also believe my consistency with this approach opened the possibility for me to receive valuable and critical feedback.

After sharing my thinking about a priority initiative and the direction I wanted to see the work move, a direct report of mine pulled me aside. She told me that I give a lot more feedback than people are accustomed to receiving and that it may be helpful to have a conversation about that so that individuals didn't misinterpret the reason I was giving them feedback. I was grateful for this colleague's feedback and immediately acted on it. She was correct that my feedback was initially viewed as being critical and concerned with their performance. Because of our conversation, I believe they could more clearly see my feedback as constructive and aimed at helping us achieve our shared objectives.

While this is just one example, there are several others where I believe people were willing to share performance challenges and problems they may not have otherwise shared because of this approach. In each instance, the insights were appreciated and used to take immediate action. Of course, not everyone adapts quickly or easily, but modeling new behaviors goes a long way toward helping others build a comfort level with change, which ultimately helps shift a culture.

Two weeks after Joelle and Victor had met to discuss Kya's progress, Mary, Sidney, and Kya arrived at the school for their parent-teacher meeting.

"Hello, Joelle," Mary and Sidney said in unison as they entered the classroom.

"Hello!" the teacher replied cheerfully as she shook their hands. "Hi, Kya." She greeted her with a smile. "How are you this morning?"

"Hi. I'm fine." Her tone was easy and matter-of-fact.

"Thank you all for coming in this morning. Have a seat, everyone," Joelle began. "We'll start the morning off with Kya's presentation of her goals, progress, and the work she is most proud of. Then we'll discuss areas for continued focus and provide time for you all to ask questions. Then, Kya will go to study hall, and we'll have time to discuss any additional questions you might have. Does that work for you?"

Mary and Sidney nodded in agreement.

Kya beamed from the beginning to the end of her presentation, and her parents watched in amazement. After struggling in school for so long, she now exuded confidence in her abilities. They smiled as she shared goals that went beyond developing proficiency in the subjects and included socio-emotional milestones around self-regulation aimed at improving her focus and leadership in the classroom. Mary and Sidney were pleased to see the progress she'd made on her classroom writing assignments.

"Kya has made remarkable progress since she began the skills center over the summer," Joelle said enthusiastically. "I'd like to take just a moment to show you a few data points." She placed a chart on the desk in front of them that showed Kya's score pre-skills center, post-skills center, and after the midterm on a reading and math skills assessment. "As you can see, she has made significant improvements!"

The widest, most beautiful smile spread across Kya's face when she saw her parents' expressions.

"That's fantastic, Kya!" Mary and Sidney congratulated their daughter enthusiastically.

"You have been doing a good job focusing on your take home assignments," Mary commented.

"Your hard work is paying off with this good report today," Sidney chimed in.

"She's doing so well. Are there areas for improvement?" Mary asked Joelle.

"There are always areas for growth, for everyone," Joelle said. "As you know, Kya has worked really hard over the last several weeks, plus the summer. She's on a good trajectory. None of her areas of improvement are at a critical phase, so let's celebrate her accomplishments today."

They all savored the celebration, and then Joelle invited Kya to go to the study hall.

When the door closed, Joelle beamed. "I couldn't be more proud of Kya if she were my own child. Let me walk you through some of the other data we track." She opened her computer and pulled up a presentation with Kya's attendance, wellness scores, school climate responses, and teacher feedback. After they discussed the additional data points, which all confirmed that Kya was thriving, she asked, "What changes have you seen in Kya at home?"

Mary responded without hesitation. "She used to procrastinate doing her schoolwork. We would have to frequently remind her and offer incentives. Now, she comes home excited to do it and organizes herself. At times, she'll get stuck and ask for help, but those times don't result in tears anymore. She is much more confident and comfortable asking questions and learning the material, even if she doesn't understand it right away."

"I'm very happy to hear that news." Noticing the time, Joelle began to close the meeting. "Do you have any other questions I can answer before we end?" She knew it was just about time for the next family, and she wanted to have a moment to capture notes from the conversation with Kya's parents and mentally shift to the conversation she needed to have with the next family. Their student was still struggling, and she knew some potentially difficult conversations were needed to determine how to best support their child.

Mary and Sidney shook their heads in unison and stood to leave. Misty-eyed, Mary hesitated and turned to Joelle. "This is incredible. Kya has struggled so much in school the last few years, and her experience here is just…amazing. Thank you."

"It's truly been my pleasure. And remember, there is a network of people supporting your daughter. I'm just the one who gets to tell you how well she's doing. I'll be sure to share your sentiments with her team."

After they left, Joelle sat back down and captured notes from her conversation with Kya's parents and reflections on the experience. While she had been a teacher for many years, it was her first time having a student take such a prominent role in presenting their work and discussing their goals. She appreciated the student advisory team's guidance in helping teachers prepare students to deliver their presentations. Joelle was quite impressed with Kya's poise and how she had used some of the presentation techniques the students practiced using fictional student data. She made a note to give kudos to the student advisory team in the central office satisfaction survey. Three students into her student conferences, with four students left on the schedule for the day, Joelle was feeling pretty good. Anticipating a more challenging conversation up next, she moved her computer aside and grabbed the notes she'd jotted for it.

The school year flew by for Chris and Kya and their parents. Before they knew it, Mary and Sidney were taking part in the kids' end-of-year exit meeting with their teachers and support teams. The purpose of the exit meeting was to review accomplishments and areas of growth during the year and set fun, aspirational learning and developmental goals for the summer.

Kya's exit interview was up first, and it was virtual due to schedule and transportation challenges.

"Hello, it's nice to see you!" Joelle greeted Mary and Sidney.

"Hi," they responded. "It's nice to see you too. Hi, Kya." They waved at their daughter, who was sitting next to her teacher in the classroom, and smiled when she waved back with a toothy grin on her face.

"We're looking forward to the report, Mary said. I apologize for having to meet virtually, but we shared with Kya that we both have work commitments that don't give us a lot of time to meet during your windows of availability."

"I understand," Joelle said. She turned to Kya. "Are you ready to share your self-assessment?"

"Yes," Kya answered quickly and with even more confidence than in the last meeting.

She pulled a sheet of paper in front of her but didn't look down and began her presentation. "I had four goals this year, and I'm excited to tell you how I did. My four goals were: One, to learn as much as possible. Two, to pay attention in class. Three, to be a good friend and teammate on my projects. And four, to keep track of my assignments."

Kya glanced at the paper occasionally, but she made sure to look at her parents on the screen most of the time.

Instead of Joelle showing the charts highlighting her progress, Kya held a piece of paper to the screen to show her progress in each of her goal areas. After she pulled the paper away from the camera, her face beamed as she looked at her parents' pleased reactions.

At the end of her presentation, Kya asked them, "Do you have any questions?"

"What helped you achieve your success?" her father asked.

Kya was prepared to answer this question because her teacher said it was a question their parents might ask. What Joelle hadn't told her was that she encouraged parents to ask a few set questions to help the children practice their presentation and planning skills when sharing information.

"Thank you for asking that question," Kya responded with a smile, having rehearsed that opening. "I'll share one example of what helped me be successful for each goal. For my learning goal, the skills center really helped me. I could understand things better there, and when I came to my school, the work was easier. I sit at the front of the classroom. I have regular breaks to run around to let some of my energy out to help me stay focused. Sometimes, I'll use a squishy stress ball. Even though it may not always look like I'm listening, I am. Ms. Ku, Victor, and my classmates tell me things that help me be a good friend and teammate. I use my notebook to help me keep track of my assignments. I don't always use it, but I use it more now than I did at the beginning of the year." Kya smiled at her teacher.

"Thank you, Kya." Joelle returned the smile.

"Nice job," Sidney encouraged.

"I'm proud of you," Mary echoed.

"I know you don't have much time today," Joelle said, "so I'll send Kya home with some suggestions for the summer and a worksheet she can use to develop one goal for the summer. It's due back to me by next Friday. Do you have any questions for me?" Joelle asked.

Kya's proud parents asked a couple of questions and shared again how pleased they were to see that Kya was performing above grade level in subjects she had previously struggled with. They hadn't expected this level of growth and shared their appreciation for Kya's experience, the sparkle that was back in her eye when she talked about school, the return of her curiosity, and the confidence she had in her ability to learn new things.

Later that week, Mary and Sidney logged in to Chris's exit meeting conversation, eager to hear their son's self-assessment. Chris joined the meeting from his computer in his bedroom. They knew he would be giving one, but he hadn't offered any hints or previews leading up to the conversation. Less concerned with his academic progress, they were eager to hear about his mental health, outlook, and overall well-being. They believed once he felt like himself again, his commitment to his academic success would return.

Chris's homeroom teacher, Mr. Wilson, welcomed Mary and Sidney, Ms. Steffan, Chris's wellness center counselor, and Mr. Lowe, Chris's student advisor. Smiles were exchanged as everyone knew each other well enough to get started with the meeting.

After Mr. Lowe reiterated the agenda to make sure everyone was on the same page, he turned to Chris and said, "Okay, Chris. Are you ready?"

Chris had come to peace with the script outline he was asked to use to prepare his self-assessment analysis. He had grown comfortable after practicing it in his room and with his student advisor and complaining about it from time to time in his student advisory.

Chris greeted everyone, then stared at the screen momentarily. Looking like he was contemplating how he could get through this assessment with the least amount of words, he took a deep breath in and exhaled long, centering himself with the practice he had learned at the wellness center. He glanced at his paper and looked back at the screen.

"Losing my mother was the worst, most difficult experience I have ever had to face." He paused and took another centering breath. "I feel like when she died, a part of me died… "

His parents burst into tears in part because, for the better part of a year and a half, they hadn't been able to get him to talk much about his feelings. This was the most he had said on the subject, and they were surprised and moved by his clarity.

"I stopped caring about things after she died." Chris paused again and glanced at his notes.

"At the wellness center, I learned a lot of things. I learned how to breathe to calm myself down when I feel sad or upset. I read a lot about death and how different cultures think about it. I could talk to Ms. Steffan about my feelings. Being around other kids going through hard things made me not feel so different because my friends all have their biological parents. At the beginning of the school year, I didn't want to go to the wellness center, but now I'm glad I did." Another pause. "I still have times when I feel sad, but I can handle it better now."

He glanced back at the notes on his desk. "This school year was better than I thought it would be. I was happy to come back to Atlanta but didn't really know if I would like the outdoor school. But I did like it—a lot!" His smile matched his tone.

"I set four goals. First, I wanted to learn more about robotics. My goal is to prepare myself to compete in the robotics competition when I get to high school. They have a competition where teams raise money and design, build, and program robots. I interviewed the high school robotics coach. He asked about my grades and told me that if I did better, I would have a really good chance of making the team. He let me come and observe some of the practices, and I attended as many as I could. Through our school mentors, I got to meet engineers from four companies that use robotics, AND I got to visit their companies. It was so cool! I wrote reports on each of them." His eyes went back to the paper with his notes on it.

"I also really like the ocean. My second goal was to learn more about conservation to protect marine life. I did interviews with some of the staff at the local aquarium and attended several of their programs. I did many of my course assignments focusing on ocean topics. It was so much more interesting than my old school. I learned the things I would have learned in my old school, but it was more fun and made more sense." He smiled gratefully at his student advisor.

"I believe I did well this year. I took feedback and used it to keep improving my work in all my classes. My third goal was to continue the mindfulness practices I learned at the wellness center and keep a journal. I did that. I set a reminder on my phone, and it helped that we practice in school and at the wellness center. Now I use the practices when I'm at home or with friends and I get upset or irritated." Chris flashed another grin, this time directed toward his wellness center counselor, who was already beaming with pride.

"My fourth goal was to become more organized. I met this goal by keeping a binder with all my assignments and notes. I was already pretty good about this, but I got better by using strategies that helped me remember to keep my binder up to date. Do you have any questions?"

Mary and Sidney asked Chris a few questions about each of his goals, which he answered confidently.

Then Chris pulled up a digital portfolio of his work, including his work at the wellness center. He explained why he chose each item and highlighted the strengths and his growth areas with each one. His homeroom teacher shared some of the feedback she had received from Chris's teachers that provided more context on the points he had shared.

"Thank you, Chris. Outstanding presentation, and we are all really happy to have been part of your team this year." Mr. Lowe congratulated Chris and invited him to sign off from the meeting. After Chris left the meeting, Mr. Lowe continued. "Chris has demonstrated a lot of initiative this school year. He is very curious and kept us on our toes as he thought of new ways to pursue his interests in robotics and conservation. While our curriculum is not dominated by the types of tests you are probably accustomed to seeing, we do have a very rigorous curriculum and incorporate the same content and skills into the assignments and lessons that Chris is supposed to learn."

The group talked further, with everyone sharing their thoughts on his progress. Before the meeting ended, Mary and Sidney thanked each of the adults who had been working to make Chris's experience a special one.

After signing off from the meeting, Mary and Sidney got up from their seats and made their way to Chris's room. "You did a fantastic job in the presentation, Chris," Mary praised.

"We're very proud of you, Chris," Sidney said, satisfaction spreading across his face.

Chris thanked them, and they talked a little longer before Mary and Sidney left to go pick up Kya from a playdate, and Chris took a break to get some fresh air.

Reflection is a Key to Creating Your Own Personal Roadmap for Transformation

Set aside 45-60 minutes to journal. Reflect, write, review, repeat.

- What feelings emerged for you as read this chapter?

- What ideas sparked for your department or system?

- In your view, in what ways does leadership help or hinder the solutions coming to mind?

Download additional questions at www.EdImperative.org

Listening to Stakeholders and Maintaining Accountability

"Yes," Kathryn Bronner said, looking at the woman who had raised her hand in the rear of the auditorium overflowing with parents and community members. Everyone was sitting at attention, whether they were in-person or at home watching virtually, waiting to hear the district's report out on year one post-transformation.

"Thank you," Mary stood up and started. "I'm very impressed by the work the district has done and how the board has worked together to transform the district. I'm curious about what has changed in how the board itself operates?"

The board members all looked to Ms. Bronner, the school board president and waited.

Realizing they wanted her to take the lead, Ms. Bronner said, "I'll start, and my colleagues can add their perspective and anything I have missed." Leaning forward slightly, she shared the answer she had prepared in anticipation of being asked this question.

"I believe there are three distinct differences in the way we approach our work. First, prior to the transformation, as a board and community, we were working hard to improve the district from our respective points of view, but there were some essentials missing: trust and connectivity."

"While we used the right words, we didn't *feel* accountable to one another for the outcomes we championed. We didn't have a structured process for examining and building trust within the system and community. Perhaps, most importantly, we realized that we didn't have the trust necessary at the board level and throughout the system or the community to have the type of leadership necessary to drive us forward. Through the transformation process, we discussed and implemented our strategy for developing, building, and restoring trust within our board relationships. This work has carried over into our relationships with district leadership and community partners."

She made eye contact with some of the representatives in the room and nodded her thanks.

"During our transformation, we went through a rigorous process in which we examined trust across our organization. We looked at more than just stakeholder perceptions. We examined the consistency of our communication and delivery practices, processes, and outcomes to determine the extent to which they engendered trust. We examined the extent to which the capabilities we relied on to support our stakeholders were adequate to meet their needs. In the end, we have a shared vision and understanding of the strategies we are using to build and strengthen trust within the school system and community at large."

Ms. Bronner glanced at her colleagues and smiled genuinely before she continued, grateful for the process that helped them get to the point where she could see them all nodding in agreement with her.

"Second, prior to the transformation, our depth of understanding, frankly, was limited. We focused on making the necessary program improvements and resource allocation, but we didn't dig deep enough to understand what it took for staff to achieve the changes we approved. As we took inventory individually and as a whole, we realized we were not disciplined enough as a board or organization to achieve the outcomes our community and we desired. When we analyzed our communications data, we realized that our efforts unintentionally added layers of work, and even undermined staff's work in some cases. When we looked at our strategic and board-approved initiatives, we had fifteen, the overwhelming majority of which were led by the same people. We were doing way too much. As we studied other trends, we realized we'd allowed our *desire* to satisfy our constituents to overshadow our *duty* to create an environment in which leaders, staff, and students can do their best work on behalf of the community."

She glanced down at her notes.

"For example, after the board analyzed our core processes, time investments, and resource allocation, we concluded that a significant number of well-intentioned yet suboptimal practices contributed to inefficient use of time. Through the transformation process, we learned that our inefficient practices eroded trust with our staff because it signaled we were more interested in having staff meet our information needs than we were in them meeting the needs of our students, teachers, and community. Now we use our time together more effectively and monitor our collective efforts to ensure our governance is additive and not contributing to staff using its time unwisely."

Her compassionate expression told the other half of the story.

"While implementation and process-related improvements are handled by staff, as a board, we started to understand that our governance role includes a responsibility to ensure we're fostering the conditions for successful implementation and that the processes are in place to achieve the outcomes we desire. We learned our actions were unintentionally contributing to the creation of a work environment where staff did not feel safe to share ideas, questions, or mistakes that could help us achieve our shared goals because they feared punishment or humiliation if their input was not welcomed. We were deeply troubled to hear this feedback and immediately went to work creating a board policy that set an expectation for the type of culture we aspired to create in our work and learning environments. Among other things, the policy requires the superintendent to periodically monitor stakeholder perceptions of climate within the system and provide the board and community with regular updates on their perceptions to ensure we have an open dialogue about our initiatives to maintain an organizational and learning culture that foster continuous improvement.

"We also created a board policy that required the superintendent to make sure the processes and procedures used to deliver services to students, teachers, and schools are written and have embedded feedback loops that empower staff, partners, parents, and students to identify improvements that are needed. A requirement in the policy is that district leadership monitors processes to ensure they are current, regularly updated, and followed. While these processes aren't approved at the board level, board members can review them after everyone who uses the processes provides feedback.

"Our policies addressing board expectations for a workplace where people are free of intimidation, retribution, and humiliation for sharing ideas and admitting mistakes had a significant impact on the way our board functioned. Redesigned processes and procedures helped everyone develop the consistency necessary for constituents to have confidence their needs will be met. It gave the board confidence that school and district staff were listening to our stakeholders and engaging them in a way where they felt they could speak candidly. Today, with more confidence in our system's responsiveness, our board meeting, workshop, and information request practices have been streamlined to ensure staff have time to do the work that needs to be done. We have a much higher organizational understanding and focus on providing the type of governance that empowers staff to implement strategic priorities and manage the processes and systems that drive our success in an effective manner. We hear fewer concerns from our parents and partners."

With a long, deep breath, she signaled that she was approaching her conclusion and possibly the most important part of what she would share.

"Finally, a key cornerstone of the way we now operate is the integration of mindfulness as a practice to support the well-being of our students and staff, and a practice for guiding the student-centered, trauma-informed approach to education. As a result of incorporating mindfulness, a "One System, One School" approach, and a commitment to clearly written stakeholder-informed processes from classrooms to the boardroom, our culture is fundamentally different. With it, our focus is now centered around creative work and learning environments that are recognized as a leading model in the field."

Ms. Bronner paused mindfully and looked at the faces of those she had committed to serve before she finished her answer.

"In my opinion, these are the three most critical differences between how our board operated then and now. As a result of these changes, our system has much greater insight on students' needs and focus on how to address them."

She found the eyes of the specific individuals with whom she had developed better partnerships and gave them a nod of gratitude.

Sensing Ms. Bonner was done with her remarks, Don Chapman, the newest board member, spoke up. "One thing I would add is that our facilitated board trainings were extremely helpful. They were focused on helping us build rapport with one another and explore common interests. It was difficult for us to hear and accept our role in creating a work environment that was not viewed as high-performing, efficient, or effective. However, our work with the System Transformation Accelerator team helped us develop a deeper understanding of the impact of our practices and move past our initial reactions. They helped us focus on identifying our shared priorities and understanding our system performance and operations in a much deeper way than we had previously, so that we can now govern more effectively. Never once did I feel there was an external agenda influencing what we were told. I always felt like the focus was on helping us use the mindfulness techniques and trust-building frameworks to better understand how to leverage the range of governance options to address performance issues we saw and develop a clearer understanding of strategies that might impact the culture we aspired to achieve.

"I agree!" The board chair and vice-chairman chimed in.

"I would be remiss," added the vice-chair, "if I didn't acknowledge the closer working relationship that we now have with our partners. I'll highlight only two now for the sake of time. They are our education association partners and our partners at the state level. Like the members on this board, before the transformation process, the state and the district were working to improve the system from their respective vantage points. Today, we work much more closely. We regularly invited these partners to participate in each step of our transformation process to ensure there is awareness, collaboration, and alignment with our direction. We also invited them to our board committee meetings and key planning sessions. I know through many conversations with Superintendent Ellis that Mr. George Abrams, president of the Phoenix Education Association, and many, many teachers throughout the system have been tireless in their participation in the transformation process. We have the kind of working relationship we've always dreamed of." The vice-chair spotted George in the auditorium and invited him to say a few words.

George took the microphone from the runner. After greeting the board and recognizing the importance of the accomplishments being shared today, he said, "This day has been a long time coming. In my heart, I knew it was possible. I'm not going to say that everything is perfect, but I do believe we are on a very good trajectory for our students, teachers, and education support professionals. Job satisfaction among our membership has never been higher. There is a buzz and an energy that is contagious. Our teachers, our members, are excited. They feel valued, respected, empowered, and well. I'm very pleased about the journey we are on and the great work being done by everyone, from our students to our staff and office professionals. I applaud you," he said, looking at the board and superintendent, "for having the courage to go down this road." As George handed the microphone to the runner, the crowd erupted in applause.

The vice-chair thanked George. As his eyes scanned the crowd, he saw their state-level partners. "I see Clifford, the district's liaison in the state superintendent's office, Barbara, the state board of education member, and some of our legislative delegates in the audience today. Cliff and Barbara, would you like to say a word? We are very grateful to the state for waiving some existing regulations that allowed us to pursue the transformation process that brings us here today."

They both stood and smiled at each other from across the auditorium. Cliff, closest to the microphone, spoke first. "Thank you. On behalf of the state superintendent, I would like to commend you for the courage, fortitude, and progress you have shown in transforming the school system. I thank you for inviting us into the transformation process. It has helped us not only become better partners with Phoenix County but also with other districts across the state. We are in much closer communication, and I cannot overstate what an important difference that has made as we contemplated and developed a number of supports and regulations for the state. Congratulations on your systemwide transformation and a very successful school year!"

Clifford turned to Barbara. After commending the board, superintendent and leadership team, and community, Barbara shared a memory. "It seems like it was only yesterday when I spoke with Evan and Kathryn about their proposed transformation process. I had several conversations with my board colleagues at the state level and with some legislators and analysts. There were lots of questions and curiosity about the process and its potential. And I'm very pleased and excited to be at this place today with very strong and promising student outcomes, healthy stakeholder relationships, and significantly better community engagement. Congratulations!"

The crowd in the auditorium applauded.

Superintendent Ellis smiled, a look of pride and determination on his face. "Thank you. We've come a long way. If we continue on this path, we will achieve our goal of preparing every student to have many post-secondary options that provide them with economic mobility and emotional well-being. One final note to share before we move on is that our one-on-one and board prep meetings are much more focused than before. In the past, they were more issue-driven. Today, they're more strategic, focusing on advancing major initiatives and work streams instead of individual issues. Staying at this higher level frees up more time for me. It also allows my leadership team to work with staff to address the concerns that have been raised. To be clear, we still have parent concerns we are addressing, but we've gotten into a healthy practice of making public the questions and complaints we receive, our approach to resolving them, and any related updates. This transparency helps to prevent lost time answering the same questions multiple times. Our consistent practice of responding gives families confidence that they no longer need to circumvent established stakeholder feedback channels to escalate issues directly to board members to get a response." Pausing to confirm others did not have additional thoughts to share, he moved to the next portion of the meeting. "At this time, I'd like to invite up our analytics team to share some of the exciting ways we are using data to provide students with better supports."

Mr. Brady, Ms. Kincaid, and Dr. Robbins from the analytics team walked up to the podium to begin their presentation on how the district is using the Department of Research and Evaluation's data more effectively to tailor solutions to students, teachers, and families.

"Our presentation today is not just about data," Dr. Robbins, executive director of research and evaluation, started confidently, a broad smile replacing his usually stern expression. "It's also about the processes that create spaces for us to capture, analyze, discuss, and respond to student needs in a timely manner based on the data aimed at improving system performance provided regularly by multiple stakeholder groups. This evening, we'll highlight data associated with three new processes: early warning systems, whole child outcome monitoring, and teaching and learning option management. Please hold your questions, and we'll answer them at the end of the presentation."

Mr. Brady jumped right in. "Through our Early Warning Indicator System, we track students' attendance, coursework, and behavior data to identify students who are falling behind, need assistance, or are missing school for significant periods or in consistent patterns. We have improved our ability to use this data by engaging community partners to support various aspects of our support strategies in each of these areas. Whether it is identifying near-peer mentors to engage and motivate students who are at risk due to attendance or coursework challenges, or connecting students with the skills center to address learning gaps, or homework support, or counseling to address behavior issues. We also provide additional supports to our staff and partners when we notice patterns where their learning needs are manifesting as student problems. For students, our supports include the skills center, wellness center, and connection to after-school enrichment opportunities. Historically, there has been a disconnect between the awareness of needs in our classrooms and schools and what our central office knows, which has caused frustration and distrust when central office hasn't been supportive or responsive enough to promptly meet educator needs. We believe this gap contributed to persistent low outcomes on school climate surveys. Particularly responses to two questions: One, "students in my classroom are focused on learning," and two, "adults in my school care if I'm not there." So this year, we implemented a weekly feedback loop aimed at closing the information gap and positioning central office to provide better supports to schools in a more timely manner. The feedback loop is a survey with three short questions: One, what area is your comment in reference to? That could be instruction, multi-tiered support services, classroom management, training/professional development, facilities, operations or parent engagement. Two, what trend are you observing? And three, what impact has the trend had or might it have?"

Mr. Brady looked up to see a good portion of the stakeholders in the room leaning forward, eagerly awaiting his next revelation.

"This survey empowers every staff person to actively contribute to our culture of continuous improvement. Without going into too much detail on the automated survey routing process, it is routed in a way that allows clarification and resolution at the lowest levels before it's captured as a trend to be analyzed. Our survey system generates a report that is reviewed weekly by department leaders, as well as our research, planning, and process teams. The planning team monitors responses to all submissions to the Early Warning Survey and works with the respective teams to conduct a rapid inquiry cycle to determine what action should be taken and then determine the urgency and prioritization with which the submission needs to be addressed. We share regular updates on issues raised, issues validated as needing resolution, as well as actions taken and planned to provide transparency and opportunity for input."

Mr. Brady smiled broadly, foreshadowing the results of this system.

"Over eighty percent of our school and classroom leaders said they believe the new feedback loop has helped improve and accelerate communication within the school and between their school and central office. With the early insights, we have been able to support students in ways that were not possible prior to the transformation."

Mr. Brady directed the audience to turn their attention to the next slide he was projecting on the screen to the left of the stage.

"I'd like to highlight a few of the more significant changes we've made since the transformation. On your way in, you should have received handouts with a lot of this information if you'd like to follow along."

Actions Taken Due to Early Insights

- provided additional training
- refined practices and tools
- offered direct support

"We added additional training for our educators, and refined some of our practices and classroom tools to ensure the school year got off to a strong start for our neurodiverse students. We also identified thousands of ninth-grade students who were not on track to graduate and have developed a range of strategies to provide direct support to them and their teachers."

Actions Taken Due to Early Insights

- retooled partnerships
- increased after-school engagement
- provided additional training

"We have identified school community partnerships that need a reset and retooling to better meet our students' needs, while increasing the number of students involved in after-school programming that meet accepted quality standards. We have also learned that our teachers need additional training on our new third-grade literacy curriculum to meet our shared expectations for students."

Mr. Brady smiled, happy that he had the privilege of relaying these results.

"These are just a few examples of the course corrections we made after increasing our system's ability to use the new feedback loop to listen, reflect, and respond. Some of the issues we knew about before our systems improvement, but we had only anecdotes and no shared language or process to determine how large a problem was. Today, we are in a much stronger position to make course corrections to meet the needs of our students, teachers, and schools.

Over ninety percent of central office teams have said that the additional data has improved their planning and responsiveness.

It has fueled their creativity in finding solutions to meet the needs of students and families with community partners where staff did not have capacity. After analyzing the data, our research team concluded that nearly two-thirds of the stakeholder feedback provided information that enhanced the Early Warning Indicators analysis and interventions that followed. Equally important, over ninety-eight percent of all individuals submitting the survey said they spent less than ten minutes completing it."

He paused to let that fact simmer in the room.

"Now Dr. Robbins will discuss our new whole child monitoring process and the data associated with it." He gathered his things, left the podium, and smiled at his approaching colleague as he moved toward his seat.

"I have the honor of sharing about whole child outcome monitoring with you." Dr. Robbins adjusted his items on the podium and began. "This year, we also are piloting a whole child outcome monitoring process where we monitor students' academic, wellness, and school-related environmental outcomes weekly, monthly, and quarterly while concurrently working with our academic, counseling, health, nutrition, and community partner teams to proactively address issues before they grow in size. For example, we capture a daily student and educator mood rating at the beginning of the day and after every class. This is an optional survey. In our training and communications with students and staff, we talk about this as an opportunity to help us determine if there are school climate and well-being trends that need to be addressed. It's also an opportunity for us to support students and staff who may not know where to go for support."

Dr. Robbins directed their attention back to the handouts and read this section word for word.

We identified:

- 5,000 students who needed counseling support and 500 staff who needed support

- 100 new teacher classrooms who needed additional lesson support to fill some gaps they had in delivering the curriculum

- 200 classrooms with teachers struggling with classroom management challenges

- 25 principals who were overwhelmed with staff transitions, parental requests, and personal circumstances

- 200 staff who were dealing with significant health issues

Dr. Robbins flipped over a page in front of him before he continued.

"Prior to this survey, we could not easily determine usage trends within stakeholder groups. This new formative data has given us greater insight while still maintaining staff's privacy where appropriate, enabling us to be proactive in our planning, tailored in our responses, and curious in our management conversations. With the new data, each of the staff represented in the examples above have received supports."

He glanced up to see what appeared to be everyone in the audience hanging on his every word.

"We also implemented the school climate survey. We have a monthly five-question school climate survey that students, educators, parents, and partners complete. Our goal is to make more significant strides in our school climate to reach climate scores above eighty-five percent in all categories. With the additional information on school climate perceptions, we were able to schedule rapid cycle inquiry, including focus groups, to investigate trends, understand concerns, and make timely adjustments aimed at addressing issues that are most frequently related to the need for training, additional communication, assistance or prioritization support, leadership, and consistent disciplinary practices. I'd like to share a few quotes from our students and teachers participating in school surveys and focus groups. These quotes have surfaced as common themes among both groups this year."

Student Feedback

"The kids in my class are more focused on learning than before. It doesn't take them as long to get quiet when the teacher starts talking."

"I like going to school so much more than I did before. It's more fun and interesting. The teachers listen better. I don't know how to describe it. It's just not boring anymore. I like learning things that prepare me for life outside of school."

"I don't see kids being bullied as much as I did before. It's like a lot of the kids who used to bully my friends are nicer and focused on other things, and the adults in my school are so much better at stopping the bullying than they were before."

"I like that when I get mad or frustrated, there's always someone there to help me calm down and get on track so I don't miss out on the things that are happening in the class."

Teacher Feedback

"I've been in the district for ten years. As a result of the transformation process we went through, I can finally say our school has a consistent strategy and process for identifying students who struggle academically and socio-emotionally."

"For years, our school did not have a clear plan of action to implement when a student struggled academically or socio-emotionally. We have one now, and it makes my job so much more enjoyable!"

"We resolve conflicts among staff faster and in a manner that is more aligned with the values we espouse. Our work environment feels healthier, and I believe we are more effective as a team."

"There are times when our school has a student or students whose needs we are not able to meet. We try everything we know to do but fall short. With the changes the district has made from partnership, culture, and access to effective practices from peer teachers, I can say with confidence that I have access to strategies and materials to support all learners in my class."

As Dr. Robbins looked up, he could see looks of satisfaction, nods of acceptance, and even a few tears on the faces of several individuals in the audience.

"If you look at this next slide, these are the results of the school climate survey. You'll see we have reached or exceeded our eighty-five percent target perception of improvements in several areas. These surveys," Dr. Robbins continued, "demonstrate the improvements we have made in changing perceptions in every school across the system in the following areas…" Dr. Robbins continued to read through the handout verbatim to ensure that all of the data was communicated.

Improvements

- **Student Belonging.** Now, over 90 percent of our students believe an adult at their school cares if they are not there.

- **Classroom Environment.** Over 85 percent of students believe students in their class are focused on learning.

- **Safety.** Over 88 percent of students feel students in their school treat other students with respect.

- **Central Office Responsiveness.** More than 90 percent of families feel the district is responsive to their input and concerns.

- **Student Supports.** Over 85 percent of teachers believe they are given the support needed to differentiate and modify instruction for their students.

- **Instructional Practice.** Nearly 100 percent of teachers answered the following survey questions with agree or strongly agree: a) I have access to strategies and materials to support all learners in my classes; b) this school has a consistent process for identifying students who struggle academically and socio-emotionally and a clear plan of action to support them when they struggle; c) I meet regularly and often with colleagues to review and discuss student data/student work.

"This year marked the first year offering students supports through the skills and wellness centers. We produce aggregate reports after each rotational period through the skill and wellness centers to highlight overall student performance trends and provide follow-up reporting until the end of the year to track the progress of each student who used the skills or wellness centers. We believe the results we achieved in our first year are promising and provide a good baseline for future comparisons. Take a look at these results listed in the handout." Dr. Robbins moved on to the next handout and began relaying the information on it.

Skills and Wellness Center Results

- 75 percent of students in the skill center achieved their goal during their initial rotation.

- 15 percent of students needed an additional rotation to achieve their goals of reaching grade level.

- 10 percent of students did not complete their rotation through the skill center for personal reasons.

- 15 percent of families whose student did not complete the entire rotation through the wellness center expressed a desire to have their child re-enroll at a later date; 10 percent of these families requested their child be re-enrolled before the year was out.

- Of the 90 percent that reached grade level through the skill center, 80 percent continued to progress at or above grade level.

- 85 percent of students completed the skill-building portion of their rotation through the wellness center.

- 70 percent of students completed the full rotation through the wellness center.

- 80 percent of students who attended the wellness center returned to their classroom at grade level.

- 60 percent of students who attended the wellness center are on track to achieve grade level by the end of the school year.

Dr. Robbins paused and smiled involuntarily at the audible rush of awe that passed through the audience.

"Additionally, we try to connect each student to at least one after-school program that sparks their curiosity and supports their ongoing development. Today, nearly two-thirds of our students have an applied learning experience, twenty percent are in a school dedicated to providing an applied learning experience, and the demand for new applied learning offerings is rising. We use data captured on the enrollment form to determine whether students are matched with enrichment opportunities that fit their interests and monitor if those experiences are going well. We can see that seventy-five percent of our students are engaged in after-school activities, forty percent are through the school and community partners, and thirty-five percent are with other community organizations. Our data shows that, on average, students engaged in after-school activities have stronger attendance, academic performance, and wellness than those not involved with extracurricular activities."

Dr. Robbins continued to share data points on school climate, student engagement, and the mood data of students who attended the skills and wellness centers. This data evoked an enthusiastic round of applause.

"Taken together, these data tools and our review processes provide us with more timely insights and the ability to create stories that help staff better connect to student adaptive *needs* being represented by the data. This has resulted in much more frequent and richer conversations about student and staff needs, as well as urgency for and curiosity about solution development."

"That completes my portion of our presentation. Now I'd like to invite Ms. Kincaid to present the final section on teaching and learning option management." As Dr. Robbins concluded, Ms. Kincaid walked toward the podium.

"Good evening, directors," said Ms. Kincaid, student learning options data manager. "During the transformation process, we created a work group focused on planning our future so that we did not stay mired in the challenges and problems stemming from the old system we had outgrown. Before the transformation, we had significant teacher attrition, low student climate scores, and wide disparities in student outcomes. After extensive research and focus groups with students, parents, and staff, we decided that providing a broader set of learning options would be the best approach to more effectively engage students. We wanted to make it easier for principals, teachers, and other district staff to create new learning options that match their strengths and interests with the strengths and interests of students. Today, we have a structure in place that helps us adapt to students' learning needs more quickly.

"Teaching and Learning Option Management is a new process we use to determine whether any students are in a schooling option that does not seem well-suited for their strengths. It's also used to empower teachers to suggest changes to existing schooling options to better meet students' needs as well as identify new, creative schooling approaches that have the potential to meet the needs of students.

"Our research team conducts a brief survey of students, parents, and leaders and data analysis to produce a report that identifies the percentage and names of students who may be in the wrong teaching and learning model for their strengths. The analysis captures student, teacher, and parent perspectives, and then looks at overall growth, effectiveness of the teacher pairing, and performance of like students across the district. This year, the report shows that ninety-eight percent of students, families, and educators believe their child is in the correct educational model. We have a process in place to capture feedback from the two percent of parents who do not believe their child is in the correct model. For one percent of those parents, we agreed and move their child to a better learning option within the first thirty days of school. For the remaining one percent of parents, we are working with them to determine how to best support their children."

She looked up to see the audience was still leaning in.

"For educators, district staff, and community members curious about proposing new schooling options, the research team held two data sessions to dig into the aggregate trends from several feedback loops, including enrollment forms and the student schooling interest portion of the school climate survey. There was strong interest in creating new learning options. Let me show you some of the results," Ms. Kincaid said as she held up the next handout.

Individuals Involved

- 100 individuals showed up for the two data sessions.
- Nearly three-quarters of the attendees were interested in learning the trends and offering improvement suggestions.
- 10 percent of the attendees were curious about opening a new school.
- The remaining individuals attended the event as a learning exercise.

"The individuals who wanted to make improvement recommendations used what they learned to participate in focus groups conducted by one of the teaching and learning option work groups, which was charged with monitoring the performance of learning models and working with teaching and learning to make recommendations. Through this process, we identified several teachers who showed a keen understanding of systems and who appeared to have the potential to advance the district's systemic priorities. We have followed up with several of them to explore their interest in getting more involved in the district's transformational efforts."

Is this really possible?

How reliable will the satisfaction survey data be? Should central office leaders have a tool for identifying which schools do not follow their processes?

The satisfaction survey data is meant to facilitate efforts to identify the areas most in need of attention across the entire system. The survey itself is not intended to reveal insights that explain the *why* behind the numbers. Once it's possible to determine the areas in highest need of discussion, focus group conversations can be used to unpack the *why* behind the numbers.

From a management perspective, central office leaders should have a process for understanding the degree to which schools are using a given process, if it is critical to producing shared insights across multiple sites. The process should be known as an experience that produces deep listening to understand what is at the root of a variation in the use of the process to drive continuous improvement rather than a process with no other purpose than to assess compliance. At the outset of using a satisfaction survey, it's most important to begin building a culture of listening to the needs of school staff and creating an environment within central office where staff do not have to feel defensive about their performance because they know they are being supported to meet the needs of students and schools.

Given the importance of these surveys in assessing the quality of actual services, I believe the survey responses should not be anonymous. The survey instrument and dialogue that comes from it have the potential to be, and should be, used as a management tool to build trust.

Given that board members are elected and often represent such different constituencies, is it realistic to think they can come together to support this new way of working that you propose?

It is! No board member can truly meet all the needs of their constituents for very long if they are not effective at engaging their board colleagues to develop solutions that everyone believes will move the entire district forward. I hope that as communities move toward transformation, they set expectations for more collaborative working relationships among elected officials and with the superintendent. These expectations will be met when board members have a clear understanding of their role and constituent expectation that they do not attempt to manage the district in place of the superintendent they hired. Reasonable people will find effective ways to govern to promote the learning and well-being of students in their community. The harm done by turnover, community animosity, and stress created by dysfunction is a disservice to students, staff, the system, and their communities in the long run.

Won't the frequent surveying of students result in survey fatigue? What's happening to all that data anyway? Who owns it?

Students crave feedback to know if they are on the right track, and so does an effective system. I believe there are ways to obtain feedback that do not produce survey fatigue, especially if it's clear that the data is being used to provide a better learning experience. District staff and partners may be stewards of the student data providing access to professionals only as much as the data helps them perform their respective roles in supporting students more effectively. Undoubtedly, there will be many more questions to address regarding data privacy, but ideally, they should not prevent students from receiving the types of supports they deserve.

Why Listening to Stakeholders Matters to Me

In my experience as deputy superintendent, I have been involved in school board decisions where board members started out divided on topics and shifted their positions because of what they learned through their discussions with district staff and constituents.

In one example, when our district was deciding whether to take part in the city's Preschool for All initiative, there was a divide on whether to participate due to many factors: space constraints, the district's role in supporting preschool given its education mandate, and the extensive resource needs that already existed in the district. Ultimately, the board voted unanimously to partner with the city to provide its high-quality Preschool for All programming in the district, but to reach this decision, we went through *eighteen* rounds of revision on our partner agreement and *fifteen* rounds of revision on the master service agreement. We had several board work sessions, some of which were contentious. We had a number of one-on-one and two-to-two board member discussions before and after work sessions. We engaged parents to speak at board meetings and called on city and community partners to speak with board members. There were meetings with city leaders and many meetings among the teams. On several occasions, the district's participation in the initiative looked bleak, but I applaud the willingness of board members to listen and be open to changing their thinking based on what they learned. I applaud the various individuals who persevered with one more call or email or outreach to continue adding data points to the collective conversation that kept individuals at the table with an open mind.

I have also been involved in school board decisions where the stakes were similarly high, but there was not the same level of external validation to support the idea, like the research available to support preschool or the understanding of how to interpret individual board member decision-making styles because of limited time together. In these instances, I believe we missed out on some important opportunities.

In another example, the district had been experiencing challenges with its enrollment projections process. Principals were getting different projections every few weeks, which in too many instances meant principals believed their building would be getting additional staff *and* losing that staff every few weeks. In addition to the frustration of getting these conflicting messages and the erosion of trust in the system that caused, another long-term risk of failing to move a staff allocation that was not supported by student enrollment is that it would reinforce inequities among the schools and potentially cause the district to spend more money than it brings in. These concerns had reached a boiling point, and the new interim superintendent was advised that the underlying processes required a comprehensive redesign to bring about desired improvements. He tasked a team to put forth a recommendation to redesign the enrollment planning process, and the team of technical experts eventually made a recommendation. We met with the board in a work session, and when we shared the recommendation, we explained it in a manner that was too technical and did not do a good enough job explaining the impact on students and communities. As a result, it resonated with board members who had more of a technical background but not with the others. I'll never forget one board member leaning over to me to ask if the superintendent supported the proposal. While I emphatically told her yes, I knew she was signaling that he had not been vocal enough in the work session. When the meeting was over, I spoke with him about it, and he remained steadfast in his desire to see the initiative move forward.

Our timeline for making a decision was tight, and there were two board members who were vocal in their strong concerns about the proposal. Having read a lot about sales, I perceived that objections were not necessarily a definitive no. Objections might reflect an individual who is engaged and actively thinking about a flaw in the proposer's plan or a lack of understanding of the customer's needs that hasn't yet been addressed. At that time, I didn't appreciate the challenge the interim superintendent was facing—having to "read the tea leaves" of the board—especially since he hoped to be retained as the permanent superintendent, which he ultimately was.

Thinking I understood the concerns after our board work session, I rewrote the board action report and resubmitted it, but the board members who had voiced concerns still had them. I scheduled some time to talk with the person who had been the most vocal, and we had a good conversation. With a better understanding of her perspective, I rewrote the document a third time and sent it to her.

Simultaneously, I had reached out to the board chair for feedback, and she was concerned about the objections her board colleagues shared. Expressing concern about my personal reputation being negatively impacted by continuing to pursue the initiative, she recommended we pull it from the board agenda. While I appreciated her looking out for me, what I knew was this: To resolve the problem in the following year, this was our only bite at the apple. If we pulled it, we would miss our window for the coming year.

Later that day, I had the scheduled call with the board member who'd had the most vocal objections. Having read the revised draft, she enthusiastically shared, "Now *this* I can sell!"

Unfortunately, the will was not there to pull the board chair and vocal member together to get the item back on the agenda, and the effort faded unceremoniously. The decision was demoralizing for the team tasked with putting forth the recommendation and contributed to the departure of one of the members.

A month or so later, the interim, now former superintendent, mentioned on two separate occasions that the board members with the most vocal objections were asking him what happened to the initiative. He shared that the board members told him they wanted to see the initiative be implemented and hadn't intended for their questions to suggest that they weren't interested in moving it forward.

The reality is that school boards make many high-stakes decisions that are at risk if there is not a clear decision-making timeline that everyone knows must be met, some thoughtful mapping of meetings that may need to occur to get a decision over the finish line, a shared understanding of board member decision-making and personality styles to avoid misreading intentions based on verbal and nonverbal cues, and a culture that allows individuals to share ideas with the fear of punishment or humiliation. With some conversation, each of these expectations can be achieved.

A parent in the front of the auditorium raised his hand. The board president made eye contact with him and said, "Yes, sir. What is your question?"

The man responded, "My question is for the superintendent. Four of my kids have gone through the district over the last twelve years and we've got eight more years to go. I've seen your predecessors come and go. They all talked about leadership. But under your administration, I see a real difference. What are you doing different?"

"Thank you for your question," Evan said as he leaned closer to the mic. "My administration values leadership like my predecessors. With the board's support, we have taken four steps that I believe have made a significant difference. First, we identified and defined the leadership and management competencies that were essential for our leaders. We communicated those requirements and what they look like in action to our leaders and managers. We set expectations around them and provided training and support to help our leaders and managers practice them. At the risk of under-communicating, we prioritized five competencies that I'd like to highlight. They are mindfulness, managing through processes, listening, results-oriented collaboration, and communications that inspire."

"Let's start with Mindfulness. Our systems are evolving as dynamic, complex organizations with high expectations, competing priorities, uneven performance across student groups, high turnover, and, in some instances, an acute lack of trust. These factors produce many stressors. In many instances, they have reduced trauma for some people while causing or triggering trauma for others. For this reason, we need our leaders and managers to be advanced in their mindfulness practices so that they can promote their own self-care and hold a productive space for their educators to model healing-centered engagement that allows students to achieve positive outcomes.

"Next, we have the Management through Systems and Process. First and foremost, our leaders and managers need to demonstrate an advanced understanding of process improvement and be able to manage through processes to ensure there is consistent delivery.

"Then, there is Listening. We need exceptional systems listeners. These individuals have the experience to hear and discern what is being said, what is not said, and what needs to be said within and across stakeholder groups receiving or delivering a program or service. These individuals demonstrate a style and practices that encourage staff to share ideas, give feedback, and admit mistakes without the fear of retaliation or humiliation.

"Next, we have the Results-oriented Collaboration. In the midst of these dynamic circumstances, we need individuals focused on obtaining results that can be achieved collaboratively and sustained systemically.

"Finally, there are the Communications that Inspire. While we have an excellent team focused on internal and external communications, we need our leaders and managers to proactively drive these conversations so their constituents are well-informed and can trust the information they receive."

Evan paused for a moment, assessing whether the gentleman who had asked the question and others in the audience seemed to be following along. Noticing most of the heads nodding, he continued.

"Second, during our transformation process, we made sure we had the right people in the right places and the right leadership foundation in place before we launched the new strategies. We had leaders and managers participate in self-assessments and three hundred sixty degree assessments. We had honest, critical conversations with leaders and managers when we noticed there was a gap between what their role required and their skill set. Where feasible, we offered training and, in other circumstances, we offered individuals different opportunities.

"Third, as shared by our board president earlier in this meeting, our board and leadership team are working closely to ensure alignment between our words and actions. We're paying closer attention to the impact our decisions have on the culture and change we want to achieve in an effort to ensure our leadership is producing the desired behavioral changes.

"Finally, we dramatically improved our internal and external communications. Perhaps one of the biggest improvements we made was developing a decision-making matrix that gives leaders, managers, staff, and the public clarity on how decisions get made, when they get made, and some insights on why the decision-making process is what it is and why it's important for it to go through the designed process. We also set expectations and trained leaders and managers on the type of communications they need to provide to keep stakeholders informed, engaged, and confident they will receive reliable information to make timely decisions to meet their constituents' expectations.

"Together, these strategies have created a continuous improvement culture that plans, tests, listens, and acts. This culture is making a meaningful and positive difference in how students, educators, partners, and communities interact. And, perhaps most importantly, these strategies are helping us achieve the outcomes we have desired for decades."

He smiled at the gentleman, very clearly satisfied with the work the district had done over the last several years. As he sat back in his chair, he briefly looked into the eyes of each board member. When he met Kathryn's, he flattened his hands against each other in a gesture of gratitude that she had taken the chance and supported him since that first phone call when he had asked for her help.

Reflection is a Key to Creating Your Own Personal Roadmap for Transformation

Set aside 45-60 minutes to journal. Reflect, write, review, repeat.

- What feelings emerged for you as read this chapter?

- What ideas sparked for your department or system?

- In your view, in what ways does leadership help or hinder the solutions coming to mind?

Download additional questions at www.EdImperative.org

The Education Imperative

Ensuring Children Thrive in School and Life

While this book shares an aspirational story of a student-centered ecosystem functioning in a more systematic and seamless way, with community partners, to meet the needs of a family with a fourth-and eighth-grade student, it is meant to start a conversation around the possibilities and processes of a similar transformation. It is also meant to inspire ordinary people to recognize the role they can play as catalysts for such transformation. With a collective effort, we can create a more coherent vision for all students from cradle to college, and we can achieve it!

A look at the vision and mission statements of each state's department of education and board of education shows a common aspirational desire to prepare students for life. There is undeniable recognition of the importance of states' visions and missions and their financial commitment to them. According to the *Digest of Education Statistics 2021*, the United States spent more than $667 billion on public pre-K through community college education. (This does not include private schools, four-year public colleges, capital expenditures/interest, or the state of California's preschools.)[28]

Given the widespread commitment to these visions and missions, and the levels of investment, one is right to wonder what is standing in the way of creating and implementing a coherent vision that results in systems that enable the kind of outcomes we desire for *all* students.

What's standing in the way?

In my opinion, the reason the covenant promising better student outcomes has not been achieved is that the systems themselves haven't yet been designed to achieve them. There is an adage that says, "Systems are designed to get exactly the results they produce." The student outcomes our current systems produce are exactly why we need to transform them, so they produce dramatically better outcomes rather than just incremental improvements.

The commentary that follows *is not about the individuals* who make up your local system but rather the policies, practices, incentives, mindsets, intentions, and organizational cultures that dictate their daily decisions and behaviors and set the conditions for how individuals handle stakeholders dealing with adversity, crisis, and difficult life circumstances. Together, they form the guardrails in which new hires operate, boards govern, and staff work to achieve their strategic goals. They influence how leaders engage with current and prospective students, parents, and partners. These are the areas wherein communities need something like The System Transformation Accelerator to help them develop a coherent approach to meeting the needs of students and staff.

Why haven't previous efforts to transform school systems taken hold? This is a complex question with a complicated answer. To be clear, school systems *have* evolved, and in my view, several aspects of school systems *have* transformed. In this particular instance, I want to focus on why transformation on a much larger scale hasn't occurred and produced consistently high outcomes for all students. As Donella Meadows in *Thinking in Systems* notes, "A system may exhibit adaptive, dynamic, goal-seeking and even self-preserving behavior,[29] which means systems aren't docile, fixed entities waiting for the proper guidance. Quite the opposite, they are dynamic living organisms that react and may seek to self-preserve in the face of uncertainty and new direction."

At the risk of grossly oversimplifying, I believe there are five foundational reasons systems haven't transformed to become ones where all students and adults thrive.

Barrier #1: Lack of Awareness, Communication, Buy-In, and Alignment. Given the large number of stakeholders, it's common for individuals to be unaware of and to get out of sync with changes that are being advanced. School system leaders often lack time, space, and resources to consistently drive transformational change internally and across stakeholder groups. For these reasons, individuals may not actively support transformation because they haven't heard compelling stories to help them fully understand it or the underlying need; they don't know what it means for their daily routines and long-term success; or they have concerns about how it will impact what they value. Without a clear change management plan, all the proposed and actual changes can be simply overwhelming. Board members may hear concerns from constituents that they have difficulty validating or ones that raise legitimate concerns that haven't been addressed. Communication, buy-in, and alignment challenges can be difficult to overcome and unintentionally contribute to feelings of mistrust when one stakeholder feels like things are moving quickly without being adequately explained or taking feedback into account. In the end, transformation is not a well-understood concept among stakeholders, and many transformation initiatives do incorporate key success factors, resulting in systems implementing good ideas that fail to achieve the desired results.

Barrier #2: Weak Infrastructure to Lead Transformation Initiatives. Within systems, there are several common and related obstacles that stand in the way of transformation. Below is a list of the barriers I believe are the most significant.

- **Capacity**. District teams have limited capacity. Half of the year, staff are focused on the current school year; the other half, they are planning for the coming school year as they complete the current school year. They do not have staff bandwidth or resources to lead, manage, and implement every aspect of a system redesign.

- **Expertise**. Similarly, school systems often do not have institutional expertise in many of the competencies essential to transformation (change management, project management, storytelling, and process redesign, to name a few) because they have not been viewed as essential to operating successful school systems. These capabilities are vital to transforming not only structures, processes, practices, information flows, and workload, but inspiring changes in the hearts and minds of the many stakeholders that use, work in, partner with, and lead the system.

- **Turnover**. Frequent turnover at the board, superintendent, central staff, and school levels often results in organizational instability, lack of strategic continuity, and frustrated stakeholders.

- **Policy Misalignment**. Local, state, and federal policies and politics often do not reflect a shared transformation agenda due to varying circumstances and leadership when policies were created, inadequate constituency building and ineffective or non-existent feedback loops to inform and drive change, and lack of transparency around decision making timelines and processes.

- **Non-existent or ineffective processes and practices**. The impact of turnover is exacerbated by the absence of intentionally-designed processes and practices that sustain strategic continuity and ensure high quality service delivery no matter what zip code a student lives in.

- **Organizational Culture and Mindsets**. Many efforts have failed due to the absence of a change management plan that carefully shifts staff and community mindsets toward those required to support new priorities. As a result, many communities across the U.S. do not have a reliable pathway for a significant number of their PK-12 students to achieve economic mobility.

When I joined the Seattle Public Schools as deputy superintendent, they had just completed their fifth year of budget reductions with a cumulative total of $115 million. Many central services had been eliminated and others drastically reduced. The challenge, in my observation, was that while the final impact had been communicated at the board level, it had not been translated into service delivery impact statements that were communicated to schools and the community. It was not communicated clearly or frequently that goals associated with previous funding levels needed to be refined to match lower funding levels. Because of the massive turnover, procedure manuals had not been updated to reflect the new approach. As a result, school principals did not know who to call within central office departments to resolve critical student needs. New central office leaders did not have procedures they could use to communicate their team's way of work and meet the disparate needs of schools. At the outset, they did not know that many of the goals they set out to achieve were no longer attainable. There was a massive problem with expectations management, and the culture was toxic and disrespectful because individuals could not get their needs met with the consistency and ease they expected. This was particularly painful, as enrollment began growing significantly during the period.

In the end, if we had supports to help us address the common barriers to transformation, we would have been much better positioned to reduce the pain and keep the focus on learning while maintaining the trust of our community.

Barrier #3: Incomplete Unit of Change Design/Inadequate Implementation Rigor. Much has been written about whether making changes at the school, district, state, or federal level will have the most impact. While school-level transformation often has the most immediate impact on students, and district-level transformation is necessary to have community-wide impact on students, decisions at the state and federal levels can quickly and unintentionally erode school and district efforts to transform practices, culture, and more by consuming time, attention, and resources.

For sustained transformation at the local level, in my opinion, the most effective unit of change is the state because its regulations govern and shape day-to-day expectations within schools and districts and their leaders' responsibility for administering federal programs. The state is best positioned to help its communities navigate state and federal policies that are misaligned with local priorities. However, simply resting the final decision at the state level is inadequate because the state is not likely to know the pulse of each city and school community. For states and their state departments of education to be truly effective at supporting sustainable performance improvements, they must be adept at partnering with school system communities to help them navigate and, where necessary, circumvent state regulations that interfere with service delivery standards and shared priorities. Ideally, states adopt or strengthen a culture attuned to encouraging top-down and bottom-up transformation and continuous improvement initiatives that foster an appropriate level of local autonomy, system coherence, and coordination that raises the overall quality of services students and families receive.

I recall several years ago, a district rolled out its teacher training in April with the goal of achieving improvements in reading/literacy the following school year. Shortly after they completed their teacher training, the state issued a mandate that the district adopt a new reading curriculum the following year and train teachers immediately. Having just completed teacher training in its locally approved curriculum weeks before the end of the school year, the district was reluctant to shift directions, and leadership asked the state for a waiver to implement the new curriculum in the coming spring instead of the fall. The waiver would ensure a greater number of teachers could be trained on the new curriculum, and bridges could be built to help draw connections, where possible, between the locally approved curriculum they were moving away from to the state-mandated curriculum. This approach, it was argued, would reduce confusion and internal animosity, which ultimately impacts students. The state refused to grant the waiver and forced the district to train and implement the new curriculum when school opened. In this example, the state did not appear to have implementation standards that valued the importance of change management, which encourages adequate planning and training before new initiatives are rolled out. It did not provide space that encouraged bottom-up engagement in decision-making, and it didn't appear to value the importance of coherent culture-building and service delivery. In the end, this lack of coherence created real tensions between teachers and principals with central office leaders. Worse, it created an environment ripe for confusion in the classroom, which put student learning at risk, which is not what the state wanted.

Barrier #4: Lack of Incentive Alignment and Inadequate Incentive Management. Given the wide range of stakeholders involved in shaping and influencing the delivery of educational services, it is imperative that all partners in the ecosystem have economic, social, and moral incentives that keep them pulling in the same direction at the right pace with their partners. A fantastic Harvard Business Review article, *Aligning the Supply Chain Incentive*, highlights the adverse consequences that can occur when incentives get misaligned. "On April 16, 2001, Cisco's, the world's largest network equipment maker, shocked investors when it warned them that it would soon scrap around $2.5 billion of surplus raw materials—one of the largest inventory write-offs in U.S. business history."[30] The company incorrectly assumed that when partners behave in their own best interests that it also maximizes the supply chain's interest. The articles goes on to note that there is considerable research showing that when companies failed to act in ways that maximized the network's outcomes, profits in this case, the supply chain performed poorly.[31]

I believe education stakeholders also incorrectly assume that when staff and delivery partners behave in their own best interest to deliver services to students and parents, it also maximizes student outcomes and system performance. In my opinion, given the wide variation in student outcomes, it is time for education systems to define and manage their supply chains. Such practices are important for education systems because there are no consistent, periodic reviews of incentive alignment in the development and delivery of core education and support services to ensure that all stakeholders have the understanding and incentive to perform in the system's best interests. Yet, in large school systems, there may be hundreds of vendor contracts and dozens of grant agreements in place, each aiming to achieve a shared objective. Relying solely on positive relationships, measures that are not causally aligned to outcomes, and a belief in the commitment of those doing the work is simply not enough to keep a system operating effectively.

A nonprofit executive and former school union leader once told me: "Charles, every provision with a collective bargaining agreement often reflects a failure between management and the union." Given the nature of incremental, interest-based bargaining, it is more likely that provisions have been added to meet the shared objectives around the district's previous leaders' visions than it is the entire agreement was created with the intention of meeting a district's new vision. My point is that with changes in administrations over the years, it's highly likely that provisions remain that are no longer relevant or aligned with the current vision (but remain because of the traditional bargaining process and competing stakeholder interests) and do not lend themselves to a periodic comprehensive review and refresh to ensure that all staff, incentives, processes, etc. are designed to optimally meet the evolving needs of students and teachers.

The collective bargaining process makes it impossible for leaders to directly engage teachers in planning and decision-making. This places union leadership in the position of being the primary interpreter of management's message and intentions to build bridges with teachers. In a politicized context, this can devolve into distortion of the district's message, resulting in an us-versus-them culture. While there are other factors to consider, this limitation makes it extremely difficult for leaders and communities to achieve transformative change. To be clear, unions have played a vital role in the workforce in this nation, and I am *not* suggesting they are not needed. I am saying, however, with respect to education, that unions, management, and communities would benefit from seeing what their incentive maps look like. I believe it is the insight needed to help achieve the breakthrough necessary to create the environments that reduce teacher burnout, elevate teacher voice, and position all students to thrive.

Barrier #5: Ineffective Performance Management and Continuous Improvement Ecosystems. Many school systems operate in an ecosystem in which numerous partner organizations do not have well-defined, rigorous performance management and continuous improvement subsystems that set delivery standards, establish and track process effectiveness for meeting the needs of each student, and use a common set of key performance indicators to monitor attainment of standards. Locally, there is often not a rigorous, independent, continuous improvement ecosystem that monitors leaders' performance and provides PK-12 education stakeholders access to independent opinions of system performance. In contrast, there is a clear ecosystem in the world of publicly traded companies. Equity research analysts cover companies and provide research that helps institutional investors determine which stocks are worth purchasing. Companies' management teams report quarterly and annual earnings. Publicly traded companies hold earnings calls to explain their performance and field questions from analysts. These insights are used to inform analysts' independent research reports. Additionally, rating agencies provide objective analysis on whether and to what degree a company's bonds are investment worthy. Strict regulations about insider information sharing create an incentive for analysts and companies to operate aboveboard.

While the above performance and improvement ecosystem is not perfect, it provides an example that, in the most basic sense, suggests independent oversight of school systems is worth considering in education, as it could increase a sense of urgency in communities, result in the development of a common set of performance measures, and cultivate consistency and accountability for the performance narrative despite turnover at the leadership and board level, among other things. For example, when a company wants to grow, it can consider a variety of funding mechanisms such as bonds (which require a bond rating to convey investment worthiness, including their ability to repay the bond) or selling shares (which results in extensive due diligence being performed to communicate a thorough analysis of the attractiveness of the stock and price to potential investors). In contrast, when a school system embarks on a new strategic plan and seeks to raise or reallocate funding to pursue it, there is no independent third-party analysis, due diligence period, or market communication that informs taxpayers or parents about the readiness of the system to receive funds. Do they have the right systems, organization, resources, strategies, and measures in place to demonstrate they can be successful? While there are no guarantees, it would be helpful to know that there has been a rigorous assessment of the district's readiness for funding before they receive their state, federal, or local tax funding. The current approach is to simply give them the money because of the importance of educational services to students and families. But there has to be a way to communicate the funding readiness of systems.

Much has been written about the perverse incentives that quarterly reporting creates with publicly traded companies. However, there is still much that can be learned by studying this model that can inform the development of a suitable improvement ecosystem in education that brings the appropriate level of transparency, urgency, transformation, continuous improvement, and accountability without creating new and unhelpful counterproductive behaviors. Given the wide disparities that exist in student outcomes, complexity of system administration, turnover of leaders, lack of requirement that school board members have large system operational experience, and gaps in administrator training, it is imperative that some structure be added to ensure an independent analysis of school systems' readiness to implement strategies that can ensure that each student's whole needs can be met. Creating a market for independent information is only possible in response to a state or federal regulation that necessitates sharing this information, or an industry practice is created that ties the analysis of this information to the release of funds. Without a predictable, common performance improvement ecosystem, there is no independent organizing mechanism or accountability to previous promises beyond the district's own efforts; politically guided federal, state, or local agenda; or privately funded organization. After decades of school systems without a performance improvement ecosystem, it's time to consider what a suitable ecosystem would look like to help support the outcomes we desire.

While a lot more can be said, at a high level, in my humble opinion, the lack of these five foundational elements are the main reasons transformational change has been so elusive and difficult to sustain. Again, this synopsis is not intended to devalue the hard work of the individuals in systems or suggest that there are not many positive examples out there. It is meant to state directly that the large-scale inequitable outcomes that exist are evidence of systems that need to be redesigned with sustained urgency and methodical precision to achieve consistently high outcomes for all students.

The Work Before Us

How does a community transition from challenges similar to those described in Phoenix County's Call to Action to a system that has resolved many of those system challenges?

Several factors must be present to set the conditions for a successful transformation.

Bridge #1: Aligned Leadership. Leadership is essential to beginning a conversation that ultimately leads to action. Some ordinary people who desire extraordinary results will need to stand up and call for change. This action will be most powerful if it is not shared with righteous indignation, but with recognition of a shared commitment to what is possible for each and every student. While leadership ultimately will be needed at the highest decision-making levels in the school system (superintendent, school board, etc.) to influence these individuals and others, mindful and performance-driven leadership must be demonstrated at every level within the system and by every stakeholder group in the community. It's imperative for the senior-most leaders to understand just how strong a mandate they have at every step of the transformation process. Parents, teachers, school and district staff, and community partners play a key role in making the mandate clear, but this clarity can only be achieved when they have complete awareness of the circumstances and decisions at hand, understanding of the implications, and assurance of transparency and active involvement along the way. Such insight will give leaders a sense of how bold they can and should be and what types of conversations they need to have to build support and commitment for change.

Bridge #2: Commitment to the Transformation Process. The superintendent, school board, and a critical mass of community leaders will need to agree to a transformation process and establish the expectations and mechanisms necessary to ensure the transformation efforts can be sustained despite any leadership turnover that may occur. They will also need to receive a waiver from the state department of education to ensure no regulations come down that will undermine the transformation process. Given the demands of the school system, it will be imperative for the superintendent and board to commit resources to allow a core dedicated district team to work on the transformation and serve as key liaisons to the day-to-day district team. This core team will be essential to building connectivity and forward momentum in each step of the transformation process because they can take their colleagues' and stakeholders' feedback, input, and concerns and ensure they are addressed while continuing to execute a process that clears a path forward to transformation.

Bridge #3: A Plan/Process for Making the Transformation. It will be imperative that a system and its core partners work with an organization that can lay out a clear process for how the district and its stakeholders will be actively involved in establishing the new vision and goals, as well as determining the sequencing of programs and services that should begin the process. It is vital that an expert bring strong administrative experience, have a deep understanding of systems, and know the ecosystem that supports students and families. Within the plan, there should be a clear process for establishing and integrating participants into an agreed-upon culture that supports the transformation process as well as structures in place to support candid dialogue, learning, informed decisions, clear decision-making processes, and action.

Bridge #4: Mindfulness, Healing-Centered Engagement, and Organizational Culture. A deep understanding of intrapersonal and interpersonal mindfulness or proficiency in its practice is critical to laying the foundation for the healing-centered engagement and creation of an organizational culture required for successful transformation. Mindfulness practices will help stakeholders focus on their self-care and develop a keener sense for recognizing when their past experiences or biases trigger certain thought patterns and behaviors that are not conducive to the leadership they wish to bring to the work environment or the transformation planning processes.

It should not be a surprise that many of the school system's stakeholders may have experienced trauma, including trauma from being punished or humiliated in response to something they said, or had their trauma activated by an interaction within the school system. After all, every breach of trust impacts the individual, despite their best efforts to mitigate the impact. Having an approach that lays the mindfulness foundation will be important in helping many stakeholders feel that it is safe to engage in the process. It will also help to ensure that individuals are treated with the care, respect, and dignity that makes them feel valued and ready to engage in the process.

It is imperative that a healing-centered approach creates the safe space for difficult conversations without losing sight of the fact that the objective of the process is to heal, restore, and strengthen the community.

Bridge #5: Sustained Urgency and Methodical Precision. School systems are dynamic organizations with priorities that can be expanded, minimized, delayed, or changed at the drop of a dime due to a variety of factors, including staff or board turnover, state or federal mandate, and when the voice of the few are loud enough to influence the board. To maintain the sustained urgency and the methodical precision that provides the continuity required to achieve system transformation, there must be a regular cadence and a consistent level of preparation to support the team(s) coming together to review status, focus on the work ahead, and discuss areas that may need more attention in order to be successful. With consistent preparation and a regular cadence, district teams should be able to overcome some of the traditional barriers to change because the transformation partner helps preserve the institutional memory, new hires are brought up to speed quickly, and the work continues to move forward with momentum.

Transformation of school systems and the state and federal agencies that support them is possible, and such a transformation can produce significantly better and more consistent student outcomes. We are long overdue for taking the sustained action necessary to achieve this goal.

Let's get to it!

Reflection is a Key to Creating Your Own Personal Roadmap for Transformation

Set aside 45-60 minutes to journal. Reflect, write, review, repeat.

- What feelings emerged for you as read this chapter?

- What ideas sparked for your department or system?

- In your view, in what ways does leadership help or hinder the solutions coming to mind?

- If this book is the only interaction you have with this vision, what one insight or idea can you take and explore to make a greater impact on students and the staff who support them?

- As individuals, we can be hypercritical about our readiness and expertise to contribute to problem-solving efforts with career practitioners and leaders. Looking back at the belief or story that you identified in A Note to the Reader, how can you rewrite that story to bring about the change you want to see in the world?

Download additional questions at www.EdImperative.org

Why Does Transforming K–12 Education Matter to Me?

The aspirational story told in *The Education Imperative* is the result of my decades-long experience in education as a student, a mentor, a teacher, a parent, and a professional determined to understand the education system from every angle and create a way to transform it into a student-centered ecosystem.

My Upbringing

I grew up in a working-class, blue-collar, Black neighborhood in inner-city Cleveland, Ohio, in the early 1970s, where neighbors monitored the kids and reported inappropriate behavior to their parents after verbally reprimanding them. Generally speaking, kids were meant to be seen and not heard in the presence of adults. It was considered disrespectful to question or fail to comply with adults' requests. While I was fortunate my parents encouraged me to have and express my opinions, I could not figure out how to express my views in a way they could be heard. I was often in trouble at school for talking back, using the wrong tone or choice of words, and not complying.

When I reflect on my childhood, I have no idea why I got into so much trouble. The only two possible reasons that make any sense to me are: one, I was always amped up on sugar, which made it hard for me to self-regulate (it's possible I was undiagnosed ADHD), and two, I had a lot of unprocessed emotions that I could not articulate as a child with what is known today as a high Adverse Childhood Experiences score. At that time, the term ACEs, a tool for measuring adverse childhood experiences, the research demonstrating their impact, and strategies for helping children experiencing them had not been developed.

Fortunately, I had many resilience factors at play.

While we had our disagreements and they needed to use every parenting tool in their toolkit, as an adult, I can say my parents were amazing! My mother was relentless at finding enrichment activities to keep me engaged and learning and building relationships with my teachers, whom I was constantly challenging. Thankfully, in a parochial school, she could call on the teachings of Jesus to prevent expulsion. At home, she frequently expressed her disappointment with tears and her disapproval with spankings and punishments, but she always asked people in our community to encourage me, soliciting my grandfather, my paper route supervisor, fellow church members, and others to give me an occasional pop-up lecture or motivational speech. Even when my parents divorced when I was in middle school, my father had a steady presence in my life. He was especially good at helping me recognize other perspectives even though it took me years to put it into practice. He was also consistent with demonstrating his love for me, which helped me keep a positive self-image.

In addition to my parents, in my inner-city neighborhood, I had very positive role models: my pediatrician, dentist, barber, and my childhood boss (manager of my newspaper route) were all Black men in my neighborhood. I had some teachers, school staff, coaches, and parents of friends who were always encouraging and supportive in ways that I can better appreciate as an adult. Perhaps more importantly, the older kids I looked up to in my neighborhood let me be me. I always felt accepted and never felt peer pressure to do anything I didn't want to do.

Obtaining a good education was always a topic of conversation in my family, and my parents were understandably concerned about my effort and future. As far as I know, none of my grandparents finished grade school. My mother was the first in her family to attend college, and my dad never forgave himself for not seizing an opportunity to test into a master's program as an adult undergraduate student. As a result, my dad only talked to me about getting a master's degree.

Even with the resilience factors at play, my future could have gone many different ways.

By the time I got to high school, I had given up. I didn't do any homework after the first few months of my freshman year, and I was in the principal's office fifty-one days out of the 186-day school year that year. Things turned around when my mother sent me to a summer enrichment and work camp where the counselors helped me see a connection between my behavior and access to a livelihood of my choosing. When I returned to school that fall, I ran for and won student body president my sophomore year and was invited to participate in Youth in Government, which I did. I also played sports, and my high school counselor helped me get a job at the mall across the street from the school. Even with all those good things going on, I did not apply myself at school and was described as apathetic.

At the end of the day, the real problem was that I didn't see where my education experience was going or how what I was learning was going to make *any* difference to me in life, and I didn't feel like my voice mattered much in my schooling experience. I felt obligated to follow a bunch of meaningless, arbitrary rules and learn things that didn't matter to me. It was during this period that my desire to create student-centered ecosystems was born—ecosystems that helped make school exciting and places where every student had access to people and environments where their talents were cultivated and they could thrive.

Meeting the Individual's Needs

When I was in college, I took part in a mentoring program aimed at supporting at-risk students, through which I met a fourth grader and his family. From the start, our relationship was two-way. It remains that way today. I would work with him on his homework, but he would *never* turn it in. His school environment was not challenging enough for him, so he wound up dropping out of school. He was attracted to the glamour of street life, got into trouble, and was placed in Job Corps. On his third day in the program, he took and passed the GED but couldn't work because he was too young.

Fortunately, my mentee also had a close and loving family who put many resilience factors in place that ultimately helped him turn his life around. While his story is a success story, I can't help but wonder if his path would have changed if he had experienced a learning environment that challenged and inspired him.

Through my relationship with my mentee, I became committed to improving the classroom experience for students so everyone's genius could be activated.

Finding the Gaps

When I left college, I was the only finance major in my class to enroll immediately in an elementary education pre-service program. Searching for a way to develop a deeper understanding of students, I worked with the Summer Bridge and Upward Bound programs. I did my student teaching in a third-grade gifted and talented classroom in Harlem and a pre-K and kindergarten class in the Coalition of Essential Schools (CES) network.

When I finished my master's program, I took a job at an alternative middle school with a new director who had an ambitious and compelling vision. Inheriting a classroom of kids who had lost their teacher a few weeks into the previous school year and completed the year with a string of substitute teachers wasn't easy. The school year started six weeks late due to an asbestos crisis, and at that time, there was no new teacher professional development. Well, if there was, I didn't receive it. Instead, a curriculum was left outside my door. Apparently, I was meant to teach myself how to support fifth- and sixth-graders whose abilities ranged from what seemed like second grade in some subjects and eighth grade in others. It was my first time administering medication and managing an environment when kids did not take their Ritalin. Given the length of time this group of promising students had been without instruction, they needed a more experienced teacher who could help them get back on track. Instead, they got a green, idealistic teacher who received no new teacher mentoring. I didn't feel set up for success and left after six weeks when I didn't feel like the school leader was being supportive. I was sick in bed for a month after the experience.

When I recovered from my disappointing experience, I set out to learn how to improve systems so no teacher would have the experience I had in the classroom.

Connecting the Dots within and across Systems

For me, connecting the dots is the result of having developed an interdisciplinary background, which I did to increase my understanding of the massive education system and its interfaces with the social systems that kids move in and out of. A recurring question for me has always been: What stands in the way of these programs and services operating interdependently and more intentionally as an ecosystem that nurtures the whole child?

My career is a mixture of interdisciplinary experiences across the domains of finance, philanthropy, and education. Throughout my education, training, and professional experience, I have moved in and out of these domains with intention.

Finance: I began my journey studying finance in college because I wanted to understand how businesses marshaled resources to innovate, grow, and improve service offerings. Working in two different roles in a Wall-Street investment bank, I learned how to research companies, pitch ideas, and distill complex topics to help investors make investment decisions and companies fuel growth and innovation.

School Districts: Inspired to improve educational opportunities, I studied elementary education in graduate school with the desire to experience the classroom and understand how teachers create learning environments that cultivate students' latent talents. Convinced that students needed more support than one teacher can give them, I eventually pursued three roles in three of the nation's fifty largest school systems, working closely with principals, central office, and civic leaders to improve services to schools. This work included supervising several departments responsible for strategic and operational execution, strengthening community partnerships, and helping parents navigate the system. As a supervisor, I regularly engaged with colleagues in research and evaluation, planning and analysis, early education application processing, Department of Technology Services, Office of Civil Rights/Title IX, project management, continuous improvement, internal auditing, data quality management, student data submissions, school choice, policy and board relations, ombudsperson/customer service, and community partnerships. In addition to my work in school districts, as a consultant I learned from a host of district leaders in large urban systems while serving on peer review teams for a membership organization where I supported them as the report drafter. I also learned from engagements I secured and led that focused on making recommendations for improvements in departments and divisions such as communications, human resources, finance, operations, instruction, technology, and operations.

Foundations: With an interest in advancing systemic reform, decentralization, and personalized learning, I pursued and fortunately secured positions in three different foundations (two national and one community). In these roles, I worked on:

- supporting grant recommendations aimed at building constituencies for school reform;
- strengthening teacher, principal, and superintendent preparation programs;
- promoting the growth of community service as a component of students' educational experience;
- expanding personalized learning, including next-generation learning, digital content and tools, and the enabling environment; and
- supporting national campus diversity initiatives, dismantling dual systems of higher education in Mississippi, and strengthening high school-to-college acceptance rates.

A Parent's Perspective: When my daughter was approaching school age, I began looking for ways that supported my information acquisition style to engage in her learning journey inside and outside of school. This type of involvement would enable me to be more involved and present as we discovered my daughter's interests and developmental needs. In my experience and conversations with parents, the process of finding the right supports is exhausting. It takes too much time, knowledge, and relationships to find, compare, and register children for programs. My wife and I have lived this reality. Too often, we were not confident we found the right opportunity for our daughter, if we could find an opportunity at all. We have found it very challenging and time-consuming to navigate the myriad opportunities and systems that exist that could support our daughter. To this end, for several years, I explored creating a parent platform that would make it easier for parents to support their child's learning and development in and out of school. Through this exploration, I developed a deep understanding of many community interfaces that support children and families, including the central library system, city and county health and human service departments responsible for foster and opportunity youth programs, housing authorities and low-income housing providers interested in increasing support to parent and student residents, as well as after-school coalitions and school system leaders interested in seeing greater youth participation in programs.

Across each of these domains and roles over the last thirty years, I have experienced different and common approaches to transformation and developed a more holistic view of what the common educational experience is and what it could be. Having seen many of the interfaces that exist between districts, community organizations, and local/state agencies, I now believe that if we look beyond the "existing walls of each organization," we will see the elements of an ecosystem that will help us fulfill the sacred contract of education.

New Characters and Roles by Chapter

Prologue

Kathryn Bonner. School Board Chair. The Board Chair has many responsibilities defined by Board policy and codified in state law. Typically, this individual plays a key role in collaborating with the Superintendent on policy issues facing the board. It is important that the two maintain an open working relationship where the superintendent can discuss matters with the Board Chair without fear of repercussion.

Evan Ellis. Superintendent. The Superintendent's responsibilities are also defined by Board policy and codified in state law. In general, the Superintendent is hired to lead and manage the school district, overseeing daily management of the schools and administration of all school board policies. The Superintendent reports to the School Board.

George Abrams. President of Local Education Association.

Clifford. The district's liaison in the State Superintendent's office.

Barbara. The district's liaison on the State Board of Education.

Chapter 1: Enrollment

Sidney Wimbush. Father/male. Biological father of Chris. Stepdad to Kya. Works at a bank.

Mary Wimbush. Mother/female. Biological mother of Kya. Stepmom to Chris. Looking for work.

Chris. Son/male. 8th grade student. Mother passed away the previous school year due to a car accident.

Kya. Daughter/female. 3rd grade female student with high energy.

Ms. Jones. Enrollment Support Team Specialist. Helps families complete their student's enrollment forms.

Dr. Niki. CEO and Founder of Mindful Leaders Project. Provides training in wellness and social-emotional learning for educators, helping professionals, and parents. Their work is rooted in the belief that healthy behavior and identity development for children is only possible when the adults who surround them have a strong capacity for self-regulation and intentional co-regulation.

Mr. Smith. Socio-emotional Learning Student Advocate. Part of a small team that receives the enrollment forms of all students who have experienced advanced trauma and ensures these students learn coping strategies and are placed in the optimal setting to support their healing and learning.

Chapter 2: Enrollment Planning in the District

Ms. Clay. Director, Multi-Tiered Support Services (MTSS) team. Leads the team responsible for connecting children to the right support academic and socio-emotional services and staff. Mr. Smith works on Ms. Clay's team.

Ms. Johnston. Executive Director, The Student Services Department. Leads the school and teacher assignment processes and oversees the MTSS team led by Ms. Clay, the master schedule process directed by Ms. Williamson, and the Student Advisory team managed by Mr. Talladesse.

Ms. Mendez. Chief Human Resources Officer. Develops and executes human resource strategy that supports the district's mission, including recruitment and training and development.

Chapter 3: Getting Ready for the Start of the School Year

Mr. Garcia. Executive Director, Learning Options. Oversees the process to pilot and introduce new learning models into the district. Works closely with Ms. Jolly who is responsible for the learning models and individuals who support school leaders.

Darren. Ms. Clay's brother who struggled as a high school student and is continuing to struggle as an adult.

Mr. Kahn. Co-Chair of the Learning Options Task Force, a volunteer group of parents, community, civic, and business leaders that provide the Executive Director for Learning Options with advice on parent communications and marketing.

Ms. Williamson. Master Schedule Process Director. Directs the process for the Master Schedule, providing guidance that enables teachers to meet more frequently with their grade-level and comparable school peers. The Master Schedule defines how learning will take place in a school by defining which teachers meet with which students, for how long, and about what subjects.

Ms. Jolly. Chief Academic Officer. Oversees all district (K-12) subject matter curricular offerings within the district.

Mr. Kim. School Community Partnerships Director. Establishes, supports, and maintains partnerships with community organizations that advance the district's multi-tiered support priorities for students.

Mr. Talladesse. Student Advisory Support Manager. Serves as a resource and facilitates the process that enables student advisor leads to share information and learn from one another. The objective of the Student Advisory is to provide students with a trusted relationship with a caring adult to help them achieve their academic and personal goals.

Chapter 4: Connecting with the School Community

Ginny. 5th grade student and Kya's new friend.

Vy. Kya's new friend.

Chapter 5: Beginning the School Year

Kevin. Friend of Chris.

Pri. Friend of Chris.

Principal Montgomery. Principal of the Outdoor School.

Mr. Lopez. Student Advisor. Leads Chris's study advisory.

Ms. Steffan, Wellness Center Counselor and Student Advisor. Acts as the liaison between students, their parents, and school advisors.

Chapter 6: The School Year

Joelle Ku. Kya's 3rd Grade teacher.

Ms. Lewis. After-Action Facilitator, 2nd Grade Teacher, Department Head.

Ms. Wilson. Principal of Kya's school.

Gary Wilson. Chris's homeroom teacher. (No relation to Principal Wilson.)

Victor. Kya's Student Advisor.

Chapter 8: Coming Together to Discuss Results

Don Chapman. New Board Member.

Mr. Brady, Ms. Kincaid, and Dr. Anderson. Analytics team. Vice Chair of the Board.

Endnotes

1 An archetype is a combined representation of needs, desires, and pain points of groups of people who share some common traits.

2 Being neurodivergent means having a brain that works differently from the average or "neurotypical" person. This may be differences in social preferences, ways of learning, ways of communicating and/or ways of perceiving the environment. Cleveland Clinic, Health Library Symptoms, https://my.clevelandclinic.org/health/symptoms/23154-neurodivergent.

3 The National Education Association identifies education support professionals as clerical services, custodial and maintenance services, food services, health and student services, paraeducators, security services, skilled trades, technical services, and transportation services.

4 "The Federal Role in Education," US Department of Education, Last modified June 15, 2021, Accessed June 2, 2021, https://www2.ed.gov/about/overview/fed/role.html.

5 The Annie E. Casey Foundation, KIDS COUNT Data Center, https://datacenter.kidscount.org/data/tables/5126-fourth-graders-who-scored-below-proficient-reading-level-by-race-and-ethnicity?loc=1&loct=1#detailed/1/any/false/1095,1729,871,573,36,867,38,18,16/10,168,9,12,185,107/11557.

6 The Annie E. Casey Foundation, KIDS COUNT Data Center, https://datacenter.kidscount.org/data/tables/7665-eighth-graders-who-scored-below-proficient-math-achievement-level-by-race-and-ethnicity?loc=1&loct=1#detailed/1/any/false/1095,1729,871,573,36,867,38,18,16/107,9,12,168,10,185/14819.

7 The Annie E. Casey Foundation, KIDS COUNT Data Center, https://datacenter.kidscount.org/data/tables/9709-children-who-have-experienced-two-or-more-adverse-experiences?loc=1&loct=1#detailed/1/any/false/1769,1696,1648,1603/any/18961,18962.

8 The Annie E. Casey Foundation, KIDS COUNT Data Center, https://datacenter.kidscount.org/data/tables/9702-children-and-teens-not-exercising-regularly?loc=1&loct=1#detailed/1/any/false/1696,1648,1603/any/18946.

9 The Annie E. Casey Foundation, KIDS COUNT Data Center, https://datacenter.kidscount.org/data/tables/5063-persons-age-18-to-24-not-attending-school-not-working-and-no-degree-beyond-high-school?loc=1&loct=1#detailed/1/any/false/2048,1729,37,871,870,573,869,36,868,867/any/11484,11485.

10 The Annie E. Casey Foundation, KIDS COUNT Data Center, https://datacenter.kidscount.org/data/tables/5116-fourth-grade-reading-achievement-levels?loc=1&loct=2#detailed/1/any/false/1095,1729,871,573,36,867,38,18,16,14/1185,1186,1187,1188/11560

11 The Annie E. Casey Foundation, KIDS COUNT Data Center, https://datacenter.kidscount.org/data/tables/5117-eighth-grade-reading-achievement-levels?loc=1&loct=2#detailed/2/2-52/false/1095,1729,871,573,36,867,38,18,16,14/1185,1186,1187,1188/11573.

12 The Annie E. Casey Foundation, KIDS COUNT Data Center, https://datacenter.kidscount.org/data/tables/5118-fourth-grade-math-achievement-levels?loc=1&loct=2#ranking/2/any/true/1729/1188/11574.

13 The Annie E. Casey Foundation, KIDS COUNT Data Center, https://datacenter.kidscount.org/data/tables/5119-eighth-grade-math-achievement-levels?loc=1&loct=2#ranking/2/any/true/1729/1188/11575.

14 The Annie E. Casey Foundation, KIDS COUNT Data Center, https://datacenter.kidscount.org/data/tables/5123-fourth-grade-writing-achievement-levels?loc=1&loct=2#detailed/2/2-52/false/13/1185,1186,1187,1188/11578.

15 The Annie E. Casey Foundation, KIDS COUNT Data Center, https://datacenter.kidscount.org/data/tables/5124-eighth-grade-writing-achievement-levels?loc=1&loct=2#detailed/2/2-52/false/18,13/1185,1186,1187,1188/11579.

16 The Annie E. Casey Foundation, KIDS COUNT Data Center, https://datacenter.kidscount.org/data/tables/6011-fourth-grade-science-achievement-levels?loc=1&loct=2#ranking/2/any/true/573/1188/12658.

17 The Annie E. Casey Foundation, KIDS COUNT Data Center, https://datacenter.kidscount.org/data/tables/5116-fourth-grade-reading-achievement-levels?loc=1&loct=2#detailed/1/any/false/1095,1729,871,573,36,867,38,18,16,14/1185,1186,1187,1188/11560.

18 Anthony Bryk, Improvement in Action: Advancing Quality in America's Schools (Cambridge, MA: Harvard Education Press, 2020),1,2, and 7.

19 Peg Thoms, "Creating a Shared Vision with a Project Team," PM Network, 11 (1), 1997, 33–35.

20 University of Washington, "Disabilities, Opportunities, Internetworking, and Technology," DO-IT, https://www.washington.edu/doit/what-difference-between-iep-and-504-plan. Accessed 11 November 2022. The Individualized Educational Plan (IEP) is a plan or program developed to ensure that a child who has a disability identified under the law and is attending an elementary or secondary educational institution receives specialized instruction and related services.

21 Ibid., The 504 plan is a plan developed to ensure that a child who has a disability identified under the law and is attending an elementary or secondary educational institution receives accommodations that will ensure their academic success and access to the learning environment.

22 U.S. Department of Education, National Center for Education Statistics, Common Core of Data (CCD), "State Nonfiscal of Public Elementary/ Secondary Education," Enrollment in public elementary and secondary schools, by level, grade, and race/ethnicity 1999–2000 through 2020–21 and 2021–22 Preliminary. (This table was prepared July 2022.

23 Digest of Education Statistics 2021, (online—Table 236.10), National Center for Education Statistics, Institute of Education Sciences, U.S. Department of Education, Washington, DC.24   Elliott, Dr. Niki. Interview. Conducted by Charles Wright, Jr. December, 15, 2022.

25 "Interest-Based Negotiation," Cambridge Dictionary, https://dictionary. cambridge.org/us/dictionary/english/interest-based-bargaining, Accessed April 7, 2023.

26 "Understanding Child Trauma," Substance Abuse and Mental Health Services Administration, US Department of Health and Human Services, https://www.samhsa.gov/child-trauma/understanding-child-trauma, Accessed August 19, 2022.

27 Carl Wiese and Ron Ricci, "10 Characteristics of High-Performing Teams," Huffington Post, May 22, 2012, Updated November 23, 2016, https://www. huffpost.com/entry/10-characteristics-of-hig_b_1536155.

28 Digest of Education Statistics 2021 (Table 236.10: https://nces.ed.gov/ programs/digest/d17/tables/dt17_236.10.asp), National Center for Education Statistics, Institute of Education Sciences, U.S. Department of Education. Washington, DC.

29 Donella H. Meadows, Thinking in Systems, E-book ed. (White River Junction, VT: Chelsea Green Publishing, 2015).

30 A supply chain includes all the activities, people, organizations, information, and resources required to move a product from inception to the customer (https://www.michiganstateuniversityonline.com/resources/supply-chain/ what-is-supply-chain-management/).

31 V.G. Narayanan and Ananth Raman, "Aligning Incentives in Supply Chains," Harvard Business Review, (November 2004), 94–102.

www.ingramcontent.com/pod-product-compliance
Lightning Source LLC
Chambersburg PA
CBHW062132040426
42335CB00039B/1969